The Art of Cyber Threat Intelligence

A Comprehensive Understanding

Crawford Thomas

Apress®

The Art of Cyber Threat Intelligence: A Comprehensive Understanding

Crawford Thomas
Leatherhead, Surrey, UK

ISBN-13 (pbk): 979-8-8688-1738-0   ISBN-13 (electronic): 979-8-8688-1739-7
https://doi.org/10.1007/979-8-8688-1739-7

Copyright © 2025 by Crawford Thomas

This work is subject to copyright. All rights are reserved by the Publisher, whether the whole or part of the material is concerned, specifically the rights of translation, reprinting, reuse of illustrations, recitation, broadcasting, reproduction on microfilms or in any other physical way, and transmission or information storage and retrieval, electronic adaptation, computer software, or by similar or dissimilar methodology now known or hereafter developed.

Trademarked names, logos, and images may appear in this book. Rather than use a trademark symbol with every occurrence of a trademarked name, logo, or image we use the names, logos, and images only in an editorial fashion and to the benefit of the trademark owner, with no intention of infringement of the trademark.

The use in this publication of trade names, trademarks, service marks, and similar terms, even if they are not identified as such, is not to be taken as an expression of opinion as to whether or not they are subject to proprietary rights.

While the advice and information in this book are believed to be true and accurate at the date of publication, neither the authors nor the editors nor the publisher can accept any legal responsibility for any errors or omissions that may be made. The publisher makes no warranty, express or implied, with respect to the material contained herein.

> Managing Director, Apress Media LLC: Welmoed Spahr
> Acquisitions Editor: Susan McDermott
> Development Editor: Laura Berendson
> Project Manager: Jessica Vakili

Distributed to the book trade worldwide by Springer Science+Business Media New York, 1 New York Plaza, New York, NY 10004. Phone 1-800-SPRINGER, fax (201) 348-4505, e-mail orders-ny@springer-sbm.com, or visit www.springeronline.com. Apress Media, LLC is a Delaware LLC and the sole member (owner) is Springer Science + Business Media Finance Inc (SSBM Finance Inc). SSBM Finance Inc is a **Delaware** corporation.

For information on translations, please e-mail booktranslations@springernature.com; for reprint, paperback, or audio rights, please e-mail bookpermissions@springernature.com.

Apress titles may be purchased in bulk for academic, corporate, or promotional use. eBook versions and licenses are also available for most titles. For more information, reference our Print and eBook Bulk Sales web page at http://www.apress.com/bulk-sales.

If disposing of this product, please recycle the paper

*"Prediction is very difficult,
especially if it's about the future."*

—*Niels Bohr*

Table of Contents

About the Author xvii

About the Technical Reviewer xix

Acknowledgments xxi

Disclaimer xxiii

Introduction xxiii

Chapter 1: The Intelligence Life Cycle—From Unknowns to Understanding 1

The Imperative of Effective Intelligence Distribution 2

The Rumsfeld Reference: Known Unknowns 4

    Phase 1: Direction..4

    Phase 2: Collection 6

    Phase 3: Processing 6

    Phase 4: Dissemination (and Feedback)...7

Chapter 2: Building the CTI Capability That Suits You 9

Leading with Clarity 12

    CTI Issues 13

    Why Routine Matters 18

    Avoiding the SOP Trap 18

    The Disruption of Endless Projects...19

    Projects vs. Programs...19

TABLE OF CONTENTS

Chapter 3: Distinguishing Technical Intelligence? 21
What Is Technical Intelligence? 21
    Why Distinction Matters 22
    L3 SOC and the Use of Technical Intelligence.......................23
    A Critical but Complementary Role 25
    Operational Observations on Implementing Technical Intelligence 25
    The Engineer vs. the Operator 25
    Operational Integration: Ownership by Users 26
    Automation and Integration: The Next Evolution....................27
    Design Intelligence for Use..28
    A Note on Scale: Intelligence Must Fit the Business 28

Chapter 4: Understanding the Cyber Landscape 31
Implications for Organizations 32
Identifying What Needs Protection 34
The Primacy of Data Protection 34
Preventing Network Intrusion 34
Steps to Protect Your Network and Data......................................35
Conclusion 36

Chapter 5: Understanding the Business 37
Understanding the Service and Operational Geography 37
Identifying Critical Data and Crown Jewels 38
Prioritizing Services and Data..38
Aligning Security Strategy with Business Priorities.......................38
From Understanding the Business to Intelligence Requirement Management...39
Step 1: Requirement Planning—What Does the Business Need to Know? 39
Step 2: Requirement Tasking—Who or What Can Answer This Question? 40
Step 3: Requirement Brokering—Executing the Intelligence Request 41

TABLE OF CONTENTS

IRM Process Diagram 42
The Art of Predictive Posturing 43
Learning from Others' Encounters 43
Preemptive Control Enhancements 43
The Virtue of Preparing for the "What Ifs" 44
The Synthesis of Response and Prediction 44
Threat Postulation 45
Conclusion 46

Chapter 6: Create the Vectors: Vector First—Actor Second 47
The Primacy of TTPs 48
The Challenge of Attribution 48
Learning from Experience 49
The "Big 5" Threat Vectors 49
Phishing 49
Malware 51
Ransomware: A Weaponized Evolution of Malware 52
    The Growth and Proliferation of Ransomware 53
    Ransomware Methodology: From Access to Encryption 53
    What Makes Ransomware Unique 54
    Detecting Ransomware 55
    Why Ransomware Matters to CTI Teams 56
    Key PIRs for Ransomware Intelligence 56
DDoS (Distributed Denial of Service) 57
Hacking 58
Insider 58
The Big 5—Understanding and Reporting Threat Vectors 60
Why the Big 5 Matters 60

TABLE OF CONTENTS

Single-Page Reporting with the Big 5 Table 61
How to Use This Table 62
The Analyst's Role in Impact and Understanding 62
Overlapping Vectors 64

Chapter 7: Geopolitics 67
Applying Geopolitical Intelligence to Cyber Threat Reporting 71
Conclusion 72

Chapter 8: Fraud 73
Key Types of Cyber Fraud 74
Ten Best Practices for Combating Cyber Fraud 75
Conclusion 78

Chapter 9: Spheres of Influence 79
The Three Spheres of Influence 79
    1. The Business Sphere (Innermost) 80
    2. The Micro Sphere (Middle) 81
    3. The Macro Sphere (Outermost) 82
Applying the Spheres of Influence in Practice 83
Conclusion 84

Chapter 10: Fusion 85
Understanding Fusion: Beyond Data Aggregation 85
The Process of Fusion: A Strategic Approach 86
Conclusion: The Essence of Fusion in CTI 87

Chapter 11: PIRs (Prioritized Intelligence Requirements) 89
Introduction to Prioritized Intelligence Requirements (PIRs) 89
Understanding Intelligence Requirements 89
The Challenge of Prioritization 90

TABLE OF CONTENTS

PIRs Focused on Threats, Not Internal Controls 91
Standing Tasks and Their Importance 91
Layering PIRs with Essential Elements of Intelligence (EEIs) 91
1. Stay Focused on the Threat 92
2. A PIR is a Question, Not a Statement 92
3. Use Essential Elements of Information (EEIs) 92
4. Prioritize PIRs and EEIs 93
5. Classify PIRs as Sensitive Information 93
6. Align PIRs with Key Threat Vectors 93
7. Establish Metrics Around PIRs 93
8. Regularly Review and Update PIRs 94
9. Incorporate Business Unit (BU) PIRs Without Bias 94
10. Label Intelligence Reports with the Relevant PIRs 94
Conclusion: The Role of PIRs in Cyber Threat Intelligence 94

Chapter 12: Intelligence Collection Plans (ICPs) 97
Populating the ICP: The Fusion of PIRs and Collection Assets 97
Understanding Collection Asset Capabilities 98
Benefits of a Well-Executed ICP 98
Conclusion: The Strategic Importance of ICPs 99

Chapter 13: Requests for Information (RFIs) 101
Conclusion 105

Chapter 14: Vendors 107
1. What Is the Budget and Are There Any Hidden Costs? 107
2. Run a Clear and Well-Thought-Out RFP 108
3. Can They Answer Specific Prioritized Intelligence Requirements (PIRs)? ... 108
4. Reputation and Proven Expertise 108

TABLE OF CONTENTS

5. Integration with Existing Security Tools and Scalability 108
6. Threat Coverage and Breadth of Intelligence 109
7. Data Accuracy and Relevance 109
8. Customization and Flexibility 109
9. Support and Service Level Agreements (SLAs) 110
10. Compliance with Industry Standards and Vendor Longevity 110
Conclusion 110

Chapter 15: Intelligence Sources 113
Ten Fundamentals of Managing Intelligence Sources 113
Applying These Fundamentals in Practice 117
Conclusion 118

Chapter 16: Internal Control Data 119
Ten Fundamentals for Leveraging Internal Control Data in CTI 120
Conclusion 123

Chapter 17: Intelligence Sharing 125
Ten Fundamentals of Intelligence Sharing in CTI 126
Conclusion 129

Chapter 18: The Cyber Criminal 131
Ten Key Considerations for Navigating the Cyber Environment 132
Ransomware: The Criminal Weapon of Choice 136
Conclusion: A Criminal Ecosystem, Not Just a Battlefield 137

Chapter 19: Scenarios for Testing 139
Ten Best Practices for Writing Cyber Threat Scenarios 140
Conclusion 143

Chapter 20: End to End Process 145

Ten Fundamentals for CTI Within an End-to-End Cybersecurity Strategy 146

Intelligence As the Catalyst in End-to-End Strategy 149

Deception As a Defensive Tactic 150

Conclusion 150

Chapter 21: Heat Maps 151

Ten Fundamentals for Using Heat Maps Effectively in Threat Intelligence 152

Enhancing Threat Heat Maps with Scenarios and Control Monitoring 154

Visualizing Control Effectiveness and Residual Risk 155

Cyber Threat Heat Map 155

Conclusion 157

Chapter 22: Inherent Threat vs. Residual Risk 159

Ten Key Points to Remember When Assessing and Reporting Inherent Threat and Residual Risk 160

Example: Phishing as Inherent Threat vs. Residual Risk 163

Integrating Inherent Threat and Residual Risk with Risk Appetite 164

Conclusion 164

Chapter 23: AI Emerging Technology 165

Understanding the Basics: AI, Machine Learning, and LLM 166

    What Is Artificial Intelligence (AI)? 166

    What Is Machine Learning (ML)? 166

    What Is a Large Language Model (LLM) 166

AI's Evolution in Cybersecurity: From ML to AI 167

The Role of Context in AI 168

The Pros and Cons of AI in Cybersecurity 169

    Pros 169

    Cons 169

TABLE OF CONTENTS

    The Evolving Role of AI Vendors 170
        AI Use Cases in Cybersecurity 171
        Agentic AI: The Next Frontier 171
        The Role of the CISO: From Gatekeeper to Digital Trust Architect 172
        Implementation Strategy 172
    Challenges in Securing AI-Driven Systems 173
    Five Best Practices for Integrating AI in Cyber Threat Intelligence 173
    The Cyber Skills Gap and the Role of AI 174
    What the Skills Gap Really Means 174
    Enter Artificial Intelligence 175
    The Gen Z Cyber Education Issue 175
    Implications and the Path Forward 176
    Conclusion 176

Chapter 24: The Attack Surface 177
    Ten Common Attack Surfaces 178
    Ten Fundamentals of Attack Surface Management 180
    Conclusion 182

Chapter 25: The MITRE ATT&CK Framework in CTI 183
    From Reference to Real-Time Relevance 184
    Why TTPs Matter More Than Actors 185
    Operationalizing ATT&CK for Detection Engineering 186
    Conclusion: Make the Framework Work for You 187

TABLE OF CONTENTS

Chapter 26: The Stakeholders 189
Core Stakeholders in the Intelligence Ecosystem 190
Business Stakeholders Often Overlooked 192
Building an Intelligence-Led Culture of Partnership 192

Chapter 27: Intelligence Report Writing—The CTI Output 195
The Art of Writing Intelligence 195
Avoiding Bespoke Overload 196
Cadence and Format of Periodical Reporting 196
Pull vs. Push Reporting Culture 197
Report Format and Consistency 197
Team Alignment and Responsibility 198
Threshold for Ad Hoc Reports 198
Conclusion 198

Chapter 28: Intelligence Maturity—Balancing Growth with Purpose 199
What Is a Capability Maturity Model (CMM)? 200
CTI Maturity Levels 200
    Level 1—Ad Hoc/Reactive 201
    Level 2—Defined, but Isolated 202
    Level 3—Integrated and Operational 202
    Level 4—Intelligence-Led 203
    Level 5—Optimized and Adaptive 203
    Applying the Model 204
Conclusion 204

xiii

TABLE OF CONTENTS

Chapter 29: The Near Future—What Else Is Going On 205

Quantum Computing: The New Crypto Threat, Without the Vendor Hysteria......205

    1. Quantum Safety Awareness Workshops 206

    2. Framing "Safety" in Safety-Critical Industries 207

    3. Governance Before Gadgets 207

    4. EU and Regulatory Timelines 208

Defense Spending and the Cyber Crossroads 208

    1. What Is the Actual Threat to the Nation? 208

    2. Where Is the Crossover Between Military and Civilian Cyber Threats? 209

    3. How Does Defense Cyber Spending Translate into Corporate Reality?.....209

    4. Cyberwar or Cybercrime? 210

Final Thought: Aligning Vision, Not Just Resources 210

Implications for Cyber Threat Intelligence (CTI) Teams 211

    1. Reframing the Threat Landscape 211

    2. Data Classification and Prioritization Intelligence 212

    3. Reporting with Precision, Not Panic 212

    4. Supporting Cross-Domain Fusion: Military and Corporate 213

    5. Internal Threat Alignment 213

    6. Preparing for Policy and Regulatory Pressure 214

Chapter 30: Final Thoughts of Significance: Lessons Beyond the Page 215

Noise, Trust, and Timeliness 215

The Stakeholder Disconnect 216

Data Models, Standards, and Sharing 216

The Economics of Threat 217

Human Factors and Training 217

Asymmetric Adversaries and Adaptive Defense 217

Technical Intelligence and Operational Control	218
The SME Reality	218
Vendor Vigilance	219
Measuring Intelligence Value	220
Threat Hunting and Campaign Tracking	220
Revisit the Big 5	221
Mitre ATT&CK and Attribution	221
Conclusion	221
Bibliography	**223**
Index	**225**

About the Author

Crawford Thomas is a former British Army officer and intelligence specialist with over 20 years of experience spanning counterterrorism, strategic intelligence, and cyber threat operations.

Commissioned from the Royal Military Academy Sandhurst, he began his career with The Argyll and Sutherland Highlanders, serving in operational roles in Northern Ireland before transferring to the Intelligence Corps. There, he led the UK's Anti-terrorist Training and Advisory Team, including a deployment to Washington following the 9/11 attacks, and conducted intelligence operations in Iraq, Afghanistan, Pakistan, and Bangladesh.

His career included leadership roles at the UK's Intelligence Collection Group (later the UK Defence Joint Intelligence Fusion Centre) and at the UK High Commission in Islamabad, where he worked to counter arms trafficking and narcotics (drugs out–guns in) networks alongside UK Special Forces and UK intelligence agencies.

After leaving the military, Crawford transitioned into financial services, joining a regional bank in Scotland before becoming Global Head of Cyber Threat Intelligence at a Swiss multinational bank. In that role, he built and led a global CTI team across three continents. Working with limited resources, he developed a capability supported by just six analysts and five intelligence vendors—all for under US$1 million a year.

Under his leadership, that bank's CTI function achieved a *"formidable"* rating in the Bank of England's CBEST assessment, the UK financial sector's threat-led testing standard. The program evaluates how effectively organizations can withstand realistic, intelligence-driven cyberattacks—making the top-tier rating a mark of exceptional maturity and preparedness.

ABOUT THE AUTHOR

Crawford's experience—across military operations, government intelligence, and corporate cybersecurity—has given him a unique understanding of the full intelligence life cycle. Today, he advises organizations on building agile, intelligence-led cybersecurity capabilities rooted in mission clarity and operational excellence.

This book represents the culmination of that journey, blending strategic insight with hands-on experience to help others build and run CTI programs that make a difference.

About the Technical Reviewer

Luca Berton is a respected AI, DevOps, Cloud, and Automation expert with over 15 years of hands-on experience in high-security environments. Luca is the author of numerous books on Kubernetes, Red Hat, and Ansible, and he has worked across high-regulated sectors to architect resilient, cloud-native infrastructure. His review helped validate the accuracy, practicality, and alignment of this book's content with today's enterprise security demands—ensuring that the guidance provided is both technically sound and operationally relevant. You can explore Luca's work at lucaberton.com.

Acknowledgments

As I write these words, I'm reminded of how far this journey has taken me—from military intelligence operations to leading global cyber threat teams. This book captures that journey, blending lessons learned in the field with the frameworks and routines needed to build a successful, intelligence-led cybersecurity program. But the insights here weren't shaped in isolation.

Special Thanks

To the leaders who trusted me to lead, learn, and question—thank you. Your influence shaped my thinking and taught me the value of integrity in decision-making.

To the colleagues I've worked alongside—military, public sector, and corporate—your commitment to clarity, challenge, and critical thinking helped refine much of what you'll find in this book.

This work is the result of collaboration, curiosity, and experience across complex and high-pressure environments. It reflects not only how cyber threats behave, but how effective CTI teams must think. If this book helps one team adopt a more focused, intelligence-led approach, it will have done its job.

—Crawford Thomas

Disclaimer

The views and opinions expressed in this publication are solely those of the author and do not reflect the views, policies, or positions of any current or past employers. All content is based on publicly available information and personal experience. No confidential or proprietary data has been disclosed.

Introduction

In the ever-evolving realm of cybersecurity, the need for robust and proactive threat intelligence has never been more critical. This book is designed to arm you with the essential knowledge and tools required to establish a world-class cyber threat intelligence (CTI) capability. I authored this book as a seasoned expert with over two decades of frontline experience in military intelligence and cyber threat intelligence within the financial sector, this guide is not just theoretical—it's a distillation of hard-earned, practical wisdom.

This book is not a typical consultation manual filled with checkboxes and generic advice. Instead, it draws from the real-world experiences of a practitioner who has navigated the complexities of regulatory pressures and excelled in environments that demand nothing less than excellence. Notably, during a recent CBEST testing, my leadership and the performance of his CTI team were described as "formidable." This recognition underscores the level of expertise and effectiveness you can expect to learn from.

You are invited on a comprehensive journey through the critical stages of building a CTI function: from developing a strategic vision, formulating prioritized intelligence requirements, and selecting the right vendors, to mastering the nuances of intelligence reporting. This book is designed to guide you in creating a CTI capability that not only protects your business but also enhances its efficacy and fosters an environment of reliability and trust—both internally and externally.

The necessity for this book stems from the current cybersecurity landscape where businesses face an increasing barrage of threats. They require impeccable IT security across all platforms, often taking risks that stretch beyond their risk appetite. Email systems, provided ubiquitously by major vendors, remain a prime target despite advanced security measures. Meanwhile, the rise of Ransomware as a Service has given a new edge to this already formidable threat, turning organizations into unwitting participants in attacks aimed at third-party applications.

This guide is indispensable because it equips you to respond to these challenges with authority and preparedness. In a world where vulnerabilities are identified daily and the threat landscape shifts with dizzying speed, having a top-tier CTI team is not just an asset; it's a necessity. If this book does not equip you to build and lead such a team—regardless of your organization's size—it has not fulfilled its purpose. Let's embark on this journey to transform your cybersecurity challenges into a testament to your strategic foresight and operational excellence.

What Is Cyber Threat Intelligence?

Cyber Threat Intelligence (CTI) is the practice of understanding the threat. It is the disciplined analysis of adversary behavior, intent, and capability—focused not on everything that could happen, but on what is likely to happen, to you. CTI looks outward, over the horizon, to identify, contextualize, and anticipate threats before they reach your environment. It draws from the perspective of the attacker to understand how, when, and why an intrusion or data loss might occur. The goal is not simply to respond to incidents, but to preempt them—by learning from what has

INTRODUCTION

happened to others, assessing the methods and motives of attackers, and aligning that knowledge with what your organization is trying to achieve, where it operates, and how it functions. Without relevance and context, information is noise; intelligence is what happens when that information is applied with the purpose of protecting what matters.

A seasoned CTI analyst, grounded in deep subject matter expertise, should be able to operate with 95% accuracy even in the absence of external sources—because real intelligence begins with understanding, not just data.

Understanding the CTI Layers

Cyber Threat Intelligence is the blend of analytical talent and experience, with contextual information used to combat cybersecurity threats. In a digital world where cyber threats evolve daily, Cyber Threat Intelligence (CTI) provides organizations—regardless of size—with a crucial advantage: the ability to stay proactive rather than reactive.[1] Whether it's *Mrs. Miggins' international flower shop* or a multinational financial institution, the need to understand whether your business is being targeted or impacted by cyber activity is essential.

The depth and sophistication of that understanding will naturally vary. It is entirely appropriate—and often necessary—for smaller businesses to adopt a proportionate approach based on their regulatory obligations, customer expectations, and available resources. In some cases, it may be enough to leverage built-in tools like Microsoft Defender for Office (MDO)

---

[1] Microsoft Security, "7 cybersecurity trends and tips for small and medium businesses to stay protected" (31st Oct 2024): "Research shows that 31% of SMBs have been victims of cyberattacks such as ransomware, phishing, or data breaches." https://www.microsoft.com/en-us/security/blog/2024/10/31/7-cybersecurity-trends-and-tips-for-small-and-medium-businesses-to-stay-protected/

INTRODUCTION

and Microsoft Defender for Endpoint (MDE) to detect and neutralize threats automatically, ensuring continuity of service with minimal intervention or analysis.

At the other end of the spectrum, large enterprises may invest in dedicated, in-house CTI teams capable of conducting deep analysis into adversary behavior,[2] evaluating threat capability, and producing tailored threat assessments. These teams contribute strategic insight to the broader security posture, support operational planning, and directly inform incident response and board-level risk decisions.

Regardless of scale, the principle remains the same: CTI is essential at every level, because understanding the threat is the first step toward managing it.

At its core, intelligence is not just about collecting data—it is the analysis of gathered information from multiple sources to create understanding. Effective threat intelligence is about synthesizing diverse information and turning it into insight that informs decisions.

An effective threat intelligence program combines open source, paid for and fellow industry sources, and transforms them into usable knowledge that helps an organization defend against everything from software application vulnerabilities to phishing[3] campaigns and advanced persistent threats. It covers three core domains: strategic, operational, and tactical intelligence. Together, these create a multilayered defense posture.

---

[2] SANS Institute, 2025 Cyber Threat Intelligence Survey (May 2025) p. 5: "Notably, more organizations than ever report having dedicated CTI teams—52% of respondents—representing an increase of 10 percentage points compared to 2018." https://socradar.io/discover-the-key-trends-shaping-cyber-threat-intelligence-in-2025/

[3] Verizon DBIR 2024: phishing (and closely related pretexting) present in 31% of breaches; median "time-to-click" < 60s. https://www.verizon.com/business/resources/reports/dbir/

It is important to note that while these layers are often defined distinctly, the boundaries between strategic, operational, and tactical intelligence can blur—especially in mature intelligence functions that understand and monitor the full end-to-end cyber process. Good intelligence frequently flows across layers, enriching all levels of decision-making.

Strategic Threat Intelligence

Strategic threat intelligence provides the high-level, long-term view essential for aligning cybersecurity with business goals. It informs leadership decisions by analyzing broader trends, threat landscapes, geopolitical developments, and emerging technologies.

Strategic intelligence supports risk posture reporting by evaluating where the business wants to go, what markets it intends to enter, and which services it will offer. It accepts that risk is part of doing business and helps articulate those risks in a way the organization can manage, rather than eliminate them.

Importantly, strategic intelligence focuses on understanding risk in context—not defeating threats. It supports a risk-informed strategy that balances operational goals with the reality of the cyber landscape. In contrast to military or law enforcement mindsets that aim to "defeat the enemy," civilian organizations must operate with the knowledge that threats cannot be eliminated, only mitigated.

Strategic intelligence also complements business strategy by enabling leadership to anticipate and plan for how threats may evolve as the business expands, pivots, or restructures. It is a lens through which business opportunity and threat exposure are evaluated side by side.

INTRODUCTION

Operational Threat Intelligence

Operational threat intelligence serves as the bridge between strategic vision and tactical action. It explores how threats materialize—focusing on the methods used by threat actors, without getting too caught up in who the attacker is. Attribution is seldom of any value, other than to satisfy the board. As within conventional warfare, cyber actors will have motivations that fall into one of the following or, on occasion, multiple categories. A simple mnemonic, MICE—Money, Ideology, Coercion, and Ego—usefully categorizes the cyber actor motivations. Operational intelligence is best served when aligned to the business units, and the cyber risks to their functionality.

A key principle is understanding that *"Bullets remain the same, regardless of who fires them."* Whether it's ransomware deployed by a state actor or a criminal group, the malware might be functionally identical. What matters is how effective the malware is, what controls stop it, and how resilient the organization is to its impact.

Operational intelligence looks for patterns across threat actor behaviors and TTPs[4] (tactics, techniques, and procedures). This enables security teams to

- Tune detections and controls
- Understand campaign-level tactics
- Prioritize responses based on likelihood and impact

---

[4] Mandiant, M-Trends 2025 Report (23rd Apr 2025) p. 10: "Stolen credentials overtook email phishing as the second most frequently observed initial infection vector in 2024, representing 16% of intrusions, compared to 14% for email phishing." https://cloud.google.com/blog/topics/threat-intelligence/m-trends-2025

Rather than expending resources on attribution, operational intelligence focuses on defense-readiness: Do we have the right armor for the bullet? This intelligence is particularly useful for aligning SOC operations and threat-hunting efforts with known adversary behaviors.

Tactical Threat Intelligence

Tactical threat intelligence is the most granular level. It addresses immediate threats with actionable data such as

- Indicators of Compromise (IOCs)
- IP addresses
- File hashes
- Malware signatures

Tactical intelligence feeds directly into SOC operations and incident response. It is proactive and reactive—helping detect current threats and prepare for the next wave based on what others have already faced.

It enables security teams to

- Detect threats in real time
- Block known malicious actors
- Tune security tools (e.g., SIEM, EDR - End point Detection and Response to the glossary at the end)

The goal is to minimize impact through rapid, data-driven action. Tactical intelligence is foundational to day-to-day cyber defense, helping defenders maintain visibility and take immediate steps to contain and mitigate incidents.

INTRODUCTION

Avoid Silo Creation

Strategic, operational, and tactical threat intelligence are not silos—they are interdependent layers of intelligence aligned to support the corresponding layer of the business. Together, they enable organizations to

- Plan long-term with awareness of emerging threats (Strategic)
- Understand and defend against broad attack patterns (Operational)
- Detect and respond to live threats in real time (Tactical)

Each layer supports a different audience—executives, SOC analysts, incident responders, and policymakers—but together they form a cohesive intelligence program.

A mature CTI capability recognizes that intelligence is not static; it is a fluid cycle of observation, analysis, dissemination, and feedback. The distinctions between intelligence types exist to define function, but in real-world applications, they often merge and reinforce one another. Understanding these distinctions—and their overlaps—is essential for building a truly intelligence-led cybersecurity function.

CHAPTER 1

The Intelligence Life Cycle—From Unknowns to Understanding

The Intelligence Life Cycle (ILC) is the fundamental framework that underpins the production of intelligence, regardless of the sector. Originally developed as a four-phase process by military intelligence organizations,[1] it has since been adopted and adapted across civilian, government, and commercial cybersecurity contexts—particularly in Cyber Threat Intelligence (CTI).

At its core, the Intelligence Life Cycle exists to formulate what an entity knows it needs to know and provide a plan to transform the unknown into a known, to a level of satisfaction that supports action or decision-making. It helps organizations move from ignorance to understanding by applying structure, direction, and method.

---

[1] US Army Field Manual 2-0 – Intelligence (1st Oct 2023), 1-30: "The intelligence process supports the activities (plan, prepare, execute, and assess) of the operations process; it is performed continuously to support each activity".

CHAPTER 1 THE INTELLIGENCE LIFE CYCLE—FROM UNKNOWNS TO UNDERSTANDING

The Imperative of Effective Intelligence Distribution

This statement highlights a key aspect of intelligence work: the need for intelligence to be seen and actioned, rather than perfecting its distribution to the extent that it risks being ignored or overlooked. This concept underscores a few pivotal elements in the intelligence process:

1. **Visibility over Perfection:** The priority should always be to ensure that intelligence reports reach recipients who can act on them, even if the distribution isn't perfectly aligned with predefined protocols. The consequences of intelligence being ignored because it was never seen are far more severe than it reaching an unintended audience within the organization who may redirect it appropriately.

2. **Encouraging a Proactive Culture:** Cultivating an organizational culture that prioritizes attention to and action on received intelligence is crucial. This involves training and sensitizing all members of the organization to the importance of the intelligence they may receive, ensuring that they understand the potential consequences of inaction. Culture creation is a leadership function. A memorable quote: "Culture eats strategy for breakfast."

3. **Feedback Mechanisms:** To avoid both errors—sending intelligence to the wrong place and ignoring intelligence—robust feedback mechanisms should be established. These mechanisms can help in continuously refining the processes of intelligence

distribution and utilization. Feedback ensures that intelligence flows are monitored and adjusted to enhance accuracy and relevance.

4. **Responsiveness to Intelligence:** There should be clear guidelines and protocols on how to respond to the intelligence received. This ensures that even if intelligence is initially misdirected, it does not go unnoticed or unacted upon. Every piece of intelligence should trigger a standard procedure of verification and action, which can significantly reduce the risk of critical information being ignored.

5. **Integration with Risk Management:** Aligning intelligence processes with the organization's risk management framework can ensure that intelligence is not only distributed appropriately but also prioritized based on the organization's risk appetite and security needs. This strategic alignment helps in making informed decisions about resource allocation and security measures.

By embracing these practices, organizations can mitigate the risks associated with overlooked or underutilized intelligence. The idea that it's better to have intelligence considered "stupidly" placed than not considered at all serves as a stark reminder of the critical importance of making sure that every piece of intelligence is given the attention it deserves. This approach not only prevents potential security incidents, but also reinforces a security-conscious mindset across all levels of the organization, ensuring a robust defense against cyber threats.

CHAPTER 1   THE INTELLIGENCE LIFE CYCLE—FROM UNKNOWNS TO UNDERSTANDING

The Rumsfeld Reference: Known Unknowns

The global public became familiar with the concept of intelligence "knowns and unknowns" during the early 2000s, when US Secretary of Defense Donald Rumsfeld famously said:

> *"There are known knowns... There are things we know we know. We also know there are known unknowns... But there are also unknown unknowns..."*

Though often parodied, this logic applies directly to the intelligence process. The Intelligence Life Cycle is designed to take "known unknowns"—the things we know we don't understand—and construct a process to investigate and close those gaps. It also accepts that there may always be "unknown unknowns" lurking outside our field of view, waiting to be discovered.

The Intelligence Life Cycle can be broken down into four phases:

Phase 1: Direction

Direction is the starting point of the intelligence process. It defines what the organization needs to know, and frames those requirements as specific, actionable questions—not vague statements. This is the orientation phase: where curiosity, risk awareness, and strategic insight meet.

In practice, Direction

- Frames questions using Priority Intelligence Requirements (PIRs)
- Filters and manages Requests for Information (RFIs)
- Ensures the questions are relevant and actionable

CHAPTER 1   THE INTELLIGENCE LIFE CYCLE—FROM UNKNOWNS TO UNDERSTANDING

CTI teams must scrutinize questions for

- Business relevance
- Feasibility of response
- Whether the question has already been answered (and where that answer is stored)

It is also during this phase that the team distinguishes between standing tasks (e.g., "Monitor the ransomware landscape") and specific taskings (e.g., "Has Lockbit 3.0 been observed in financial services this week?").

Importantly, questions must be documented—both answered and unanswered—to enable institutional knowledge and avoid duplication. RFIs and PIRs often overlap, and the CTI team should manage that interplay to maintain clarity and efficiency.

The Direction phase is not a one-time event. It is in constant motion, reacting to incoming intelligence, changing threat landscapes, and incident data. It may be triggered by

- A phishing incident in the SOC[2]
- An alert from an endpoint tool
- External reports from industry peers[3]

Direction feeds the rest of the cycle—but it also continuously returns to the top. The ILC, therefore, is not a static cycle—it behaves more like a cyclone.

---

[2] Cisco Talos Incident Response, IR Trends Q1 2025: Phishing soars as identity-based attacks persist (28th Apr 2025): "Threat actors used phishing to achieve initial access in 50% of engagements, a notable increase from less than 10% last quarter." https://blog.talosintelligence.com/ir-trends-q1-2025/

[3] Verizon, 2024 Data Breach Investigations Report—News Release (1st May 2024): "More than two-thirds (68%) of breaches involve a non-malicious human element." https://www.verizon.com/business/resources/reports/dbir/

Think of the Intelligence Life Cycle as a cyclone: constantly rotating, drawing in new signals, and generating force. At the top, the spinning momentum keeps each phase active, while also creating pressure to absorb more intelligence questions from across the environment.

Phase 2: Collection

Once Direction has shaped the requirements, Collection involves identifying and leveraging the appropriate assets to gather the data. These might be

- Vendor intelligence feeds
- Open-source intelligence (OSINT)
- Internal telemetry (e.g., SOC logs, endpoint detections)
- Law enforcement or industry sharing groups

The collection should be targeted, not random. The asset selected must match the type of question posed. A well-run CTI team knows its tools and their strengths. If an asset to answer the PIR doesn't exist, this must be acknowledged as a capability gap—and flagged to leadership for potential future investment.

Collection is not just about gathering volume—it is about precision, corroboration, and timeliness.

Phase 3: Processing

Processing is the transformation of raw data into a product. This includes

- Corroborating sources
- Deconflicting overlapping information
- Extracting meaning and pattern
- Writing and formatting for the end user

Some frameworks split "Processing" and "Analysis" into separate phases, but a four-phase model keeps things simple and integrated.

Processing is where the analyst constructs the intelligence product:

- **Situation**: What happened?
- **Analysis**: Why did it happen, and what does it mean?
- **Recommendations**: What actions should be taken?

Style guides and standard formatting are vital. Readers should always know what to expect.

Phase 4: Dissemination (and Feedback)

Dissemination is the distribution of the final intelligence product to the right audience. But this phase is more than just delivery—it includes

- Grading and classification
- Choosing the right communication channel (e.g., email, briefings, dashboards)
- Ensuring timeliness and accessibility

Equally important is **feedback**. Feedback loops confirm

- Whether the intelligence was received
- Whether it was useful
- Whether it prompted action

CTI teams do not chase outcomes—but they must make it easy for consumers to report on outcomes. Dissemination must connect—it must touch the right part of the business and result in meaningful awareness or change.

CHAPTER 1   THE INTELLIGENCE LIFE CYCLE—FROM UNKNOWNS TO UNDERSTANDING

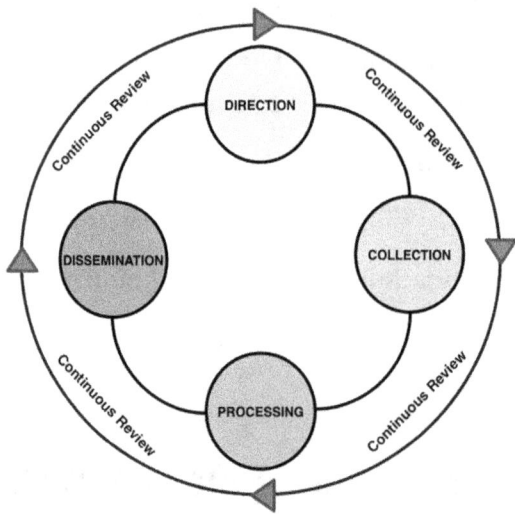

Figure 1-1. *The intelligence life cycle*

I often refer to the "Intelligence Life **Cycle**" as the "Intelligence Life **Cyclone**." Just as a cyclone must make landfall to have an effect, the Intelligence Life Cycle must deliver its product to the right consumer at the right time. Intelligence that never lands—never influences—is wasted energy.

The Intelligence Life Cycle is continuous, fluid, and powerful when run properly. From Direction to Dissemination, it provides a blueprint for turning uncertainty into action.

CHAPTER 2

Building the CTI Capability That Suits You

Building a world-leading CTI Capability is a multifaceted endeavor that requires strategic foresight, tactical planning, and a nuanced understanding of both the cyber threat landscape and the operational environment of your organization. Here are ten fundamental things to consider when assembling and operating such a team:

1. **Casting the Right People**: The foundation of any effective CTI team is its people. Recruit individuals who not only possess technical acumen, but also demonstrate strong analytical skills, creativity, and the ability to think like an adversary. They must be journalistic and have an enquiring mind. These things can't always be taught. Diverse backgrounds in cybersecurity, military intelligence, and law enforcement can enrich the team's perspective.

2. **Buying the Correct Vendors**: Vendor selection is crucial. Invest in solutions that offer comprehensive, actionable intelligence and not just data. The right

vendors should provide tools that integrate well with your existing infrastructure and enhance the team's capabilities to detect, analyze, and respond to threats.

3. **Be Part of the Cybersecurity Strategy**: The CTI team should be intricately linked with the broader cybersecurity strategy of the organization. This alignment ensures that intelligence activities are directly supporting the organization's security goals and risk management framework.

4. **Have Simple Processes:** Complexity often leads to inefficiency. Design processes that are straightforward and repeatable. This clarity will allow the team to focus on analyzing threats rather than navigating procedural hurdles.

5. **Read Intelligence a Lot:** Continuous learning is key in a field as dynamic as cybersecurity. The team should be encouraged to regularly consume and analyze intelligence from a variety of sources to stay ahead of new threats and tactics.

6. **Know Where Your Intelligence Needs to Go:** Intelligence should be actionable and directed toward the stakeholders who can act on it. Understanding who needs what information and when they need it is critical for the effectiveness of the intelligence life cycle.

7. **Work Seamlessly with the SOC and Control Owners:** Collaboration with the Security Operations Center (SOC) and other control owners ensures that intelligence is integrated into the operational response. This cooperation is vital for proactive rather than reactive security posture.

CHAPTER 2   BUILDING THE CTI CAPABILITY THAT SUITS YOU

8. **Remember, Intelligence Is Nothing Without the "So What?":** Intelligence must always be contextualized with an analysis of its implications. Every piece of intelligence should be accompanied by an explanation of why it matters to the organization and what should be done about it.

9. **Have Experts, Not Generalists:** While a broad understanding of cybersecurity is important, true value comes from having analysts with deep, domain-specific expertise in key threat vectors—such as malware, phishing, DDoS, insider threats, or geopolitical cyber activity. These specialists bring critical insight that generalists simply cannot replicate. Accurate and timely intelligence reporting—at all levels (strategic, operational, and tactical)—relies on this vector-level expertise.

   An analyst focused solely on reporting tactically or strategically, without a grounded understanding of the threat vector itself, will inevitably produce incomplete assessments. Their reports may lack context, nuance, and most importantly, a credible "so what?"—the commentary that links technical threat data to real-world business risk.

   A single tactical event—such as an unusual PowerShell execution or phishing email—can have strategic consequences, potentially triggering shifts in risk appetite, regulatory exposure, or customer trust. The ability to trace this impact across the CTI life cycle, and articulate it clearly, is what defines a true threat vector expert.

Experts don't just know the "what"; they understand the "why" and "how"—and that insight is what turns threat data into decision-ready intelligence.

10. **Have a Routine:** Establish a regular routine for intelligence gathering, analysis, dissemination, and feedback. A predictable routine not only ensures consistency in operations, but also helps in quickly identifying when an anomaly occurs.

In a discipline as dynamic and demanding as Cyber Threat Intelligence (CTI), consistency is a rare commodity—but an essential one. Establishing and maintaining a structured daily routine anchored by clear Standard Operating Procedures (SOPs) offers analysts a foundation from which to operate effectively and confidently.

Leading with Clarity

What CTI teams need is

- A leader with operational experience
- A defined plan of what the CTI team delivers, to whom, and when
- A minimal-fuss implementation of tools and processes that support output, not bureaucracy

In summary, a good routine isn't a rigid checklist—it's a disciplined flow. SOPs provide the scaffolding. Analyst insight breathes life into it. Leaders should protect the routine, not disrupt it with excessive experimentation. The best intelligence teams are those that operate like a well-run program: consistent, purposeful, and quietly effective.

CHAPTER 2   BUILDING THE CTI CAPABILITY THAT SUITS YOU

By focusing on these ten key areas, you can build a CTI team that not only protects your organization, but also positions it as a leader in the cybersecurity community. This approach ensures that your team stays agile, informed, and prepared to counter sophisticated cyber threats.

CTI Issues

In the rapidly evolving cybersecurity landscape, CTI teams face a myriad of challenges that could potentially impede their effectiveness and operational efficiency. As we delve deeper into the future of CTI, it's critical to address the top issues that could shape the dynamics of these teams. Here is an exploration of the top ten issues facing CTI teams going forward:

1. **Intelligence Is Often Seen As a Luxury:** In many organizations, CTI is still not viewed as a fundamental aspect of cybersecurity but rather as an optional, high-end add-on. This perception can lead to insufficient funding and support, hindering the team's ability to perform its essential functions.

2. **Vendor Costs Are Increasing:** As cyber threats become more sophisticated, the tools and services needed to counter them also become more advanced and, consequently, more expensive. Rising vendor costs can strain budgets, especially in economically uncertain times.

3. **False Positives Rates Cost Time:** High rates of false positives in threat detection systems can drain CTI resources, diverting attention from real threats and reducing overall efficiency. Minimizing false positives remains a significant challenge for CTI teams.

4. **SOCs Struggle to Gain External Intelligence Context:** While Security Operations Centers are crucial for the day-to-day monitoring of threats, they often lack the broader context that CTI can provide. Bridging this gap is essential for a holistic security posture.

5. **Businesses Reducing Headcount:** Economic pressures and budget cuts can lead to reductions in staff, impacting CTI teams disproportionately. Smaller teams may struggle to cover all necessary aspects of threat intelligence, from data collection to analysis and response.

6. **Hard to Retain the Team:** Retaining skilled cybersecurity professionals is increasingly challenging due to a competitive job market and high demand for experienced personnel. CTI teams often face high turnover rates, which can disrupt continuity and knowledge retention.

7. **AI Is Answering Intelligence Questions:** The rise of artificial intelligence in cybersecurity can be a double-edged sword. While AI can enhance the capabilities of CTI teams, it also raises concerns about the over-reliance on automated systems which might miss nuances that a human analyst would catch.

8. **CISO's Strategies Are Focused on Risk, Not Threat—Fusion Remains a Dream:** There's often a disconnect between CISO strategies, which are typically risk-averse, and the proactive threat hunting required in CTI. This misalignment can prevent the integration of CTI into broader security strategies, making effective fusion of information and resources a distant goal.

9. **Controls Come with Intelligence Services:** Many cybersecurity controls now come bundled with their own intelligence services. While beneficial, this can lead to fragmentation and siloing of critical threat data, complicating the threat landscape rather than clarifying it.

10. **Everyone's an Expert:** The democratization of cybersecurity knowledge and tools has led to a proliferation of self-proclaimed experts. This can result in conflicting information and approaches, making it difficult for CTI teams to maintain clarity and authority in their operations.

Addressing these challenges requires a concerted effort from both CTI professionals and organizational leaders. It involves redefining the value of intelligence within the cybersecurity framework, investing in the right tools and talent, and fostering an environment where CTI is integrated seamlessly with broader security operations. By confronting these issues head-on, organizations can enhance their defensive posture and better prepare for the cyber threats of the future.

CHAPTER 2 BUILDING THE CTI CAPABILITY THAT SUITS YOU

As we progress through the complexities of establishing and operating a successful CTI team, it is crucial to understand three fundamental concepts that underpin the effectiveness of cybersecurity operations. These concepts not only guide how CTI teams function but also clarify their role within the broader security architecture of an organization.

1. **Risk Is Not the Same As Threat**

    Understanding the distinction between risk and threat is pivotal. Risk refers to the potential for loss or damage when a threat exploits a vulnerability. Essentially, it is about the possibilities of what might happen within your environment due to your specific exposures and the safeguards you have (or have not) put in place. Conversely, threat is about the capabilities and intentions of the adversaries targeting you. A threat exists outside of your control and represents what the adversary can and is willing to do. CTI focuses on identifying and understanding these external threats, enabling the organization to assess and mitigate risks more effectively.

2. **The Role of Intelligence Is to Disseminate Information**

    The primary function of a CTI team is the collection, analysis, and dissemination of intelligence. It is crucial to understand that once this intelligence is handed over to operational teams—such as the Security Operations Center (SOC) or incident response teams—the CTI team's direct involvement with how this intelligence is used should generally cease. The operational teams are responsible for acting on the intelligence, whether that involves adjusting security controls, conducting further investigations, or implementing strategic changes. The CTI team should focus on providing the most accurate and actionable intelligence possible but not on managing its application.

3. **Intelligence-Led Approach Is a Moment in Time**

   Adopting an intelligence-led approach means prioritizing the use of intelligence to guide security decisions and responses. However, this does not imply that intelligence should always lead the operation throughout its entirety. Intelligence serves as a critical starting point that informs and shapes the initial stages of planning and response. As the situation develops and new information becomes available—either through ongoing operations, additional intelligence, or changing adversary tactics—the lead can shift. Operational teams might take over as the situation demands tactical responses that are outside the typical purview of the CTI team.

By embracing these fundamentals, readers can better appreciate the nuanced roles and responsibilities of a CTI team within their organization. These principles help delineate the boundaries of CTI work and underscore the dynamic interplay between intelligence and operations in cybersecurity. As the threat landscape continues to evolve, so too must our strategies for addressing and mitigating these threats, always informed by a clear understanding of these underlying concepts.

Continuing from these foundational concepts, it's essential to underscore the importance of precise intelligence distribution within an organization. This principle is vividly captured in a remark made by a highly respected senior intelligence officer: "To send intelligence to the wrong place is stupid, to ignore intelligence is incompetence, I'd rather have stupid." This aphorism serves as a critical lesson in the management and utilization of intelligence within cybersecurity operations.

CHAPTER 2   BUILDING THE CTI CAPABILITY THAT SUITS YOU

Why Routine Matters

Routine brings rhythm. It gives structure to complexity and helps analysts understand what is expected of them. A well-defined daily cadence—incorporating monitoring, triage, reporting, collaboration, and feedback—builds maturity and dependability into CTI operations. More importantly, it allows analysts to focus their cognitive effort on threats and problem-solving rather than repeatedly deciding what to do next.

When paired with SOPs, routine can

- Enhance repeatability and reliability of tasks
- Ensure coverage across threat vectors
- Enable cross-team handoffs and shared understanding
- Provide a framework for onboarding and training

But like any tool, SOPs must be applied with care.

Avoiding the SOP Trap

Over-engineering SOPs—making them overly complicated or bureaucratic—creates risk. The best analysts thrive on clarity and intuition. If your SOPs become too rigid or convoluted, you'll push away the very talent you need. Analysts may become fearful of deviating from the script—even when critical thinking is required.

Intelligence work demands agility. SOPs should enable, not inhibit. They should

- Be clear and actionable, not academic
- Define what good looks like, not just process steps
- Allow for analyst judgment and professional interpretation

The Disruption of Endless Projects

Another threat to routine is the proliferation of internal projects. Too many organizations unknowingly sabotage their CTI routines by overloading teams with projects that draw analysts away from their core responsibilities.

Projects are often misunderstood as a form of progress or change management. In practice, they can become a distraction—consuming time, fracturing team focus, and eroding operational consistency.

Too frequently, projects mask a leadership gap: a lack of clarity about what needs to be done, prompting the formation of large working groups and exploratory initiatives rather than decisive action. This happens when leaders don't have the operational depth to enact change themselves.

Projects vs. Programs

Understand the distinction:

- Projects are temporary efforts to produce change.
- Programs are sustained, structured approaches to deliver output over time.

CTI should operate like a program—delivering intelligence continuously, predictably, and with measurable output. That program should be underpinned by a solid routine.

CHAPTER 3

Distinguishing Technical Intelligence?

Within a mature Cyber Threat Intelligence function, the question often arises: *Should technical intelligence be treated as a distinct category, or is it simply part of the wider CTI process?* The answer lies in understanding the specific utility, users, and life cycle of technical indicators within an organization's defensive posture.

What Is Technical Intelligence?

Technical intelligence typically refers to highly granular, machine-consumable data, such as

- **Indicators of compromise (IOCs)**: IP addresses, domain names, file hashes
- **Signatures and rulesets**: YARA rules,[1] Snort/Suricata signatures, Sigma rules
- **Malware artefacts**: File paths, mutexes, registry keys

---

[1] https://yara-rules.github.io/blog/

- **Protocol-level observables**: HTTP User-Agents, C2 patterns, TLS fingerprints

- **Sandbox data**: API call sequences, code behaviors, static/dynamic analysis outputs

This kind of intelligence is often time-sensitive, high-volume, and actionable by automated systems—particularly within the Security Operations Center (SOC) and detection engineering teams.

It is distinct from strategic, operational, and even tactical intelligence in its scope and purpose. Where strategic intelligence informs business risk decisions, and operational intelligence maps out threat actor behavior over time, technical intelligence answers a simple but vital question: *What do I block, detect, or investigate—right now?*

Why Distinction Matters

Treating technical intelligence as a separate, but integrated, component of CTI has key benefits:

1. **Audience-Specific Relevance**

   Technical indicators are most relevant to SOC teams, incident response, and detection engineers—not executive leadership or business units. By distinguishing technical intelligence, CTI teams can ensure it is formatted, delivered, and prioritized correctly.

2. **Automation Compatibility**

   Unlike narrative assessments, technical intelligence can feed directly into security tooling—SIEMs, EDRs, firewalls, and threat intel platforms (TIPs). This level of integration requires accuracy, proper expiration management, and frequent validation to prevent alert fatigue or performance degradation.

3. **Temporal Sensitivity**

   Technical indicators have a short shelf-life.[2] IP addresses change, domains are recycled, and malware hashes evolve through obfuscation or repackaging. Failing to treat technical intelligence as a rapidly perishable product leads to outdated controls and missed threats.

L3 SOC and the Use of Technical Intelligence

Level 3 (L3) SOC analysts are typically the most advanced tier within a SOC, often overlapping with CTI in responsibility and skillset. Their use of technical intelligence is a crucial bridge between detection and investigation.

L3 analysts use technical intelligence to

- Validate alerts and triage escalated cases
- Enrich cases with threat context (e.g., MITRE, TTPs, malware families, threat actor links)
- Tune detection rules and SIEM correlations
- Reverse-engineer malware samples or de-obfuscate payloads
- Provide feedback to the CTI team on the utility or gaps in indicators received

---

[2] Dark Reading, "'Short, Brutal Lives': Life Expectancy for Malicious Domains" (1st Oct 2018): Longitudinal study of 23.8 million domains found a median malicious-domain lifespan of 4 hours 16 minutes. https://www.darkreading.com/threat-intelligence/-short-brutal-lives-life-expectancy-for-malicious-domains

CHAPTER 3   DISTINGUISHING TECHNICAL INTELLIGENCE?

This operational loop between CTI and L3 SOC analysts ensures that intelligence is not simply received, but **used**, **tested**, and **refined**.

Five best practices for managing technical intelligence include

1. **Tag and Label Clearly**: Use metadata such as confidence, source, expiry, and associated TTPs.

2. **Use a Threat Intelligence Platform (TIP)**:[3] Automate ingestion, de-duplication, validation, and distribution to security tools.

3. **Avoid Indicator Bloat**: Not all indicators are useful. Prioritize those tied to active campaigns or targeting your sector.[4]

4. **Align with MITRE ATT&CK**:[5] Map indicators to techniques and sub-techniques to provide context and build detection logic.

5. **Establish Feedback Loops**: Ensure SOC and engineering teams report back on hits, false positives, or usefulness.

---

[3] SANS Institute, 2025 Cyber Threat Intelligence Survey (May 2025) p. 11: "Reports are followed by TIP integrations (72%), emails/slide decks (68%), and briefings (61%) as preferred dissemination methods."

[4] SANS Institute, 2025 Cyber Threat Intelligence Survey (May 2025) p. 2 Executive Summary: "CTI teams heavily favour external intelligence inputs: 90% collect external data vs. 64% that use internal sources." https://socradar.io/discover-the-key-trends-shaping-cyber-threat-intelligence-in-2025/

[5] MITRE Corporation, MITRE ATT&CK®: "A globally accessible knowledge base of adversary tactics and techniques." https://attack.mitre.org/techniques/enterprise/

A Critical but Complementary Role

While technical intelligence is a subset of CTI, it deserves distinct treatment. It is not intelligence in the strategic sense, but intelligence in the defensive sense—delivering actionable data that allows for real-time protection, detection, and response.

For CTI teams, recognizing the distinction enables better stakeholder alignment, streamlined operations, and more impactful delivery. For the SOC, it ensures that intelligence is not abstract—it's practical, usable, and relevant.

Done well, technical intelligence forms the frontline of cyber defense, powered by the depth and foresight of a true intelligence-led security model.

Operational Observations on Implementing Technical Intelligence

Deploying technical intelligence capabilities is not solely a matter of ingestion and integration. It requires clarity on ownership, purpose, and operational design. A recurring challenge within many organizations is that those who build the tools are not the ones who operate them. This is more than an IT or resourcing issue—it's an intelligence issue.

The Engineer vs. the Operator

Technical engineering teams often own the tools used for technical intelligence collection and defense. They are responsible for deploying the Threat Intelligence Platform (TIP), maintaining the SIEM, tuning EDR, and managing firewall or DNS-layer integrations. These engineers are usually removed from day-to-day operational threat detection.

CHAPTER 3   DISTINGUISHING TECHNICAL INTELLIGENCE?

While their build is honorable and often technically robust, **engineers build resilience**, **not necessarily insight**.

Think of the engineer building a wall to defend the citadel. It is thick enough to stop cannonballs and high enough to repel arrows. But when the CTI analyst asks: "How many cannonballs hit the wall? How fast were they traveling? Are they evolving?"—there's no answer. The wall wasn't designed to measure impact, only to withstand it.

This disconnect creates a dangerous blind spot. Without visibility into adversary interaction with defenses, intelligence becomes speculation.

Operational Integration: Ownership by Users

The solution is to shift responsibility for tooling functionality to the users—the CTI analysts and L3 SOC operators who need the data, not just the infrastructure.

Where possible:

- Engineers should be embedded within the SOC or CTI team structure.

- Tooling and tuning should be governed by intelligence objectives, not just engineering blueprints.

- Engineering output should be measured by data relevance, not just system uptime or deployment milestones.

This mirrors military doctrine: engineers are attached to the fighting force, but they are not the fighting force. The mission is not building the bridge; the mission is defeating the enemy across the river. The build is a means, not the end.

Automation and Integration: The Next Evolution

As technical intelligence matures, its automation and integration become crucial differentiators. Indicators must not sit in a spreadsheet or static feed—they must move.

A modern technical intelligence workflow should

1. **Correlate internal and external data:** An IOC seen internally must be checked against known malicious observables outside the network.

2. **Contextualize alerts:** A detected IP address is meaningless until mapped to MITRE techniques, campaigns, or actor profiles.

3. **Feed tools dynamically:** TIPs must push enriched IOCs directly to detection technologies—EDR, SIEM, firewall—without analyst intervention.

If the CTI team cannot automatically link a malicious file hash detected internally with its wider relevance externally, they are not delivering intelligence—they are handling raw data.

The **Threat Intelligence Platform (TIP)** is the nerve center of this capability. When well-integrated into the SIEM and SOC stack, it enables

- De-duplication and validation of IOCs
- Threat scoring and expiry management
- Contextual enrichments and tagging
- Bi-directional flows between internal detections and external threat feeds

CHAPTER 3   DISTINGUISHING TECHNICAL INTELLIGENCE?

Design Intelligence for Use

At the heart of technical intelligence success lies a simple principle: design for the user, not the builder. Engineers must enable; analysts must guide. The systems must serve the mission—not the other way around.

By embedding technical intelligence into the operational heartbeat of the SOC and CTI functions—governed by those who rely on it—you move from static defense to dynamic, intelligence-led security operations.

A Note on Scale: Intelligence Must Fit the Business

Not every organization has a CTI team. Many don't have a SOC, or even an MSSP. For countless small and medium-sized enterprises (SMEs), the idea of deploying TIPs, ingesting custom feeds, and layering detections over MITRE may feel far removed from daily operations.

And that's okay.

> *For Mrs. Miggins' International Flower Shop, threat intelligence doesn't need to be a program—it needs to be a service. She doesn't want reports or dashboards. She wants assurance: that if a threat was seen, it was blocked or deleted. And that her business continues to bloom the next day.*

This is the reality for the majority of global businesses. Intelligence at this scale is about effectiveness, not elegance. It's about outcomes, not optics.

Vendors, MSSPs, and security providers serving SMEs must ensure their services focus on

- Detection, deletion, and confirmation
- Clear, automated response without jargon
- Simple assurance, not overwhelming metrics

CHAPTER 3   DISTINGUISHING TECHNICAL INTELLIGENCE?

Whether defending a global bank or a flower shop, the mission remains the same: detect, respond, and keep the business moving.

Cyber threat intelligence must never lose sight of its purpose: to inform action, support resilience, and serve the business—whatever its size.

CHAPTER 4

Understanding the Cyber Landscape

Explore the ever-evolving nature of cyber threats and how they shape the security environment. This chapter sets the foundation for recognizing the dynamics of cyber threats.

The escalating costs of cyber-attacks underscore their prominence as a global threat, with recent analyses aligning to project an alarming trend in both frequency and impact. According to the 2023 World Economic Forum's Global Risks Report,[1] cybersecurity firmly stands among the top ten global risks today and in the foreseeable future. This recognition is indicative of the broader understanding that cyber threats are not merely isolated IT issues but pivotal economic and security challenges on a global scale.

Adding to the urgency is the projection by Cybersecurity Ventures that the cost of cybercrime will surge to an annual $10.5 trillion by 2025.[2]

---

[1] World Economic Forum, Global Risks Report 2023 (11th Jan 2023) p. 6: "Cybercrime and cyber-insecurity entered the top-10 global risks, ranked 8th for both the two-year and ten-year outlooks." https://www.weforum.org/publications/global-risks-report-2023/

[2] Cybersecurity Ventures, quoted in Business Standard, "Cybercrime costs to hit $10.5 trn by 2025" (24th Jul 2024): "Cybersecurity Ventures predicts that global cybercrime costs will grow by 15% annually, reaching $10.5 trillion by 2025." https://www.business-standard.com/finance/personal-finance/cybercrime-costs-to-hit-10-5-trn-by-2025-how-insurance-may-save-your-biz-124072400476_1.html

CHAPTER 4   UNDERSTANDING THE CYBER LANDSCAPE

This staggering figure highlights the exponential growth in both the sophistication and volume of cyberattacks, suggesting that the financial impact of cybercrime could become one of the most significant drains on the global economy in the coming years. This projected cost includes direct damages, theft of intellectual property, embezzlement, fraud, post-attack disruption to the normal course of business, forensic investigation, restoration and deletion of hacked data and systems, and reputational harm.

Moreover, Gartner's prediction that 45% of global organizations will experience a supply chain attack within the next two years underscores a shift in attack vectors.[3] Supply chain attacks represent a sophisticated threat vector where attackers target less secure elements in the supply network to gain access to better-guarded targets. This type of attack not only affects the directly targeted organization but also cascades through the supply chain, amplifying the damage and costs across multiple organizations.

Implications for Organizations

The implications for organizations facing cyber threats are many:

1. **Risk Management**: Organizations must prioritize cyber risk management equivalent to financial, operational, and reputational risk management. Incorporating robust cybersecurity strategies into corporate risk assessments and business continuity planning is no longer optional but a necessity.

---

[3] Gartner projection, cited in Ivanti, "Why You Can't Afford to Ignore Software Supply Chain Attacks" (5th May 2025): "45% of organizations will have experienced a software supply-chain attack by 2025, triple the 2021 figure." https://www.ivanti.com/blog/software-supply-chain-attack-risk

2. **Investment in Cybersecurity**: The financial implication of potential cyberattacks necessitate significant investment in cybersecurity infrastructure and capabilities. This includes not only technology but also skilled personnel and continuous employee training.

3. **Supply Chain Security**: Given the predicted rise in supply chain attacks, organizations must extend their cybersecurity protocols to include suppliers and partners. Rigorous security assessments and enforcement of security standards across the supply chain will be essential.

4. **Cyber Insurance**: As the costs associated with cyber incidents soar, cyber insurance becomes a critical component of risk management strategies. However, organizations must also be aware that insurance is not a substitute for robust security measures.

5. **Global Collaboration**: The international scope of cyber threats demands global cooperation in cybersecurity initiatives. Sharing threat intelligence, best practices, and collaborative efforts in cyber incident response can significantly enhance collective cyber resilience.

The projections from respected global entities like the World Economic Forum, Cybersecurity Ventures, and Gartner illustrate a critical juncture in the fight against cybercrime. As these threats evolve, so must strategies to mitigate them. Addressing these risks effectively will require a concerted, comprehensive approach that integrates technological, procedural, and strategic elements at all levels of the organization and across its external interfaces.

CHAPTER 4   UNDERSTANDING THE CYBER LANDSCAPE

In any discussion about cybersecurity, the most fundamental concept to grasp is that understanding the threat landscape is inherently tied to knowing what your business needs to protect. For a cyber defense strategy to be effective, it must be meticulously aligned with the specific needs and assets of the business.

Identifying What Needs Protection

The following steps can be taken to protect your network and data:
At the core of any business are its assets. These can be tangible, such as hardware and physical infrastructure, or intangible, like data and intellectual property. Among the most critical assets are company and client data. These encompass everything from sensitive personal information to financial records and proprietary business insights.

The Primacy of Data Protection

Data is not just an asset; in many ways, it's the lifeblood of modern business. Protecting this data is crucial not only for compliance with various data protection regulations but also for maintaining customer trust and business reputation. A breach involving client data can lead to severe legal penalties, loss of customer confidence, and significant financial damage.

Preventing Network Intrusion

The first line of defense in protecting these assets is to secure the network. Network intrusion attempts are among the most common threats that businesses face today. These can range from opportunistic attacks by novice hackers to sophisticated breaches orchestrated by organized cybercrime groups.

Steps to Protect Your Network and Data

1. **Risk Assessment**: Start with a thorough risk assessment to identify the most valuable assets and the most vulnerable points within your network. This involves understanding both the architecture of your network and the data flows within it.

2. **Layered Security Approach**: Implement a layered security strategy that includes firewalls, intrusion detection systems (IDS), and intrusion prevention systems (IPS). This multilayered approach ensures that even if one security measure fails, others will still be in place to thwart an attack.

3. **Regular Updates and Patching**: Keep all systems up-to-date with the latest security patches. Many network intrusions exploit vulnerabilities for which patches exist but have not been applied.

4. **Employee Training**: Since many attacks start with phishing or other forms of social engineering, training employees to recognize these threats is critical.

5. **Incident Response Plan**: Finally, have a robust incident response plan in place. This plan should include procedures for isolating affected systems, communicating with stakeholders, and recovering lost data.

Conclusion

By understanding what needs protection within your business—focusing primarily on company and client data—and taking proactive steps to prevent network intrusions, you create a strong foundation for your cybersecurity strategy. This not only protects your assets but also upholds your business's integrity and trustworthiness in the eyes of your clients.

CHAPTER 5

Understanding the Business

Delve into how business operations and cybersecurity must align to protect assets effectively. Understanding the organization's core processes is crucial for tailored cybersecurity.

In the realm of cybersecurity, one of the foundational principles is a comprehensive understanding of the business you are tasked with protecting. As a cybersecurity analyst, this knowledge is not merely helpful—it is indispensable. Understanding the nature of the business, the services it provides, its operational geography, and the data it deems critical is the cornerstone upon which a robust and effective security strategy is built.

Understanding the Service and Operational Geography

A business's service offering is its interface with the world—it is what customers see, interact with, and depend upon. As such, the cybersecurity measures that protect these services must be tailored to their unique characteristics and to the expectations of the users. The geographic footprint of the business further complicates this landscape. Different regions come with different threats, regulations, and vulnerabilities.

CHAPTER 5   UNDERSTANDING THE BUSINESS

Operating in a global arena means that one must be cognizant of a myriad of diverse cybersecurity landscapes and be prepared to navigate and comply with a complex patchwork of international laws and standards.

Identifying Critical Data and Crown Jewels

Data is often categorized into varying degrees of sensitivity and importance. As a cybersecurity professional, distinguishing between routine information and the "crown jewels"—the most critical data of the organization—is crucial. This could include proprietary technologies, customer information, strategic plans, or trade secrets. These are assets that, if compromised, could cause irreparable harm to the business's competitive position, financial stability, and reputation.

Prioritizing Services and Data

Every business has limited resources; thus, prioritization becomes a key strategy. Knowing which services are the lifeblood of the organization allows cybersecurity efforts to be focused on where they are most needed. Similarly, understanding which data is most vital enables security professionals to allocate resources effectively and ensure that the strongest defenses protect the most sensitive assets.

Aligning Security Strategy with Business Priorities

An informed security strategy uses the knowledge of priority services and critical data to deploy the best tools where they will have the greatest impact. This involves a judicious mix of preventive measures, such as firewalls and encryption for the most vulnerable software, and detection and response tools like intrusion detection systems (IDS) and security information and event management (SIEM) systems for monitoring. By doing so, cybersecurity does not become a blanket applied uniformly over the enterprise; rather, it is a custom-tailored suit of armor, strongest at the points of greatest need.

In summary, a cybersecurity analyst must understand the business inside and out—its services, its data, and its priorities—to defend it effectively. This intimate knowledge ensures that the security strategy is not only robust and comprehensive, but also finely tuned to the organization's specific risks, obligations, and objectives. Only then can a security posture be deemed truly fit for purpose, offering the best protection where it matters most.

From Understanding the Business to Intelligence Requirement Management

Understanding the business is fundamental to effective Cyber Threat Intelligence (CTI). But knowing the business, its systems, and its reliance on Internet-connected infrastructure is only the beginning. The CTI analyst's responsibility is not limited to understanding how the business functions—it is to translate that understanding into action through structured planning, prioritization, and tasking. This is where the Information Requirement Management (IRM) process begins.

Step 1: Requirement Planning—What Does the Business Need to Know?

The first obligation of a CTI analyst is to break down business understanding into prioritized intelligence requirements. It's not enough to say, "We know the business uses cloud collaboration platforms." The analyst must determine what the business needs to know to protect those systems and where those needs vary across different business units.

This involves engaging stakeholders, understanding their risk tolerance, identifying what systems or data are most critical to them, and translating that into a list of Prioritized Intelligence Requirements (PIRs). This is not a one-off process—it requires time, interviews, internal workshops, and a clear understanding of how different units measure risk, performance, and operational impact.

Once collected, these requirements must be ranked. Not all intelligence needs are equal. Some may relate to existential threats (e.g., ransomware affecting core systems), while others may be of lower priority (e.g., industry trends in phishing tactics). Prioritization ensures limited collection resources are focused where they are needed most.

Step 2: Requirement Tasking—Who or What Can Answer This Question?

Once PIRs are established, the next step is to apportion them to the most appropriate collection assets or teams. This is called requirement tasking.

Each PIR should be matched to a collection method or intelligence source that is best positioned to answer it. This could be a

- Intelligence sharing community across industry
- Internal SOC data, Threat Intelligence Platform or Commercial threat intelligence feed
- Law enforcement or government agencies
- OSINT tool or dark web monitoring platform

This step should not be difficult in a mature intelligence function. The assets in place—whether procured via an RFP process or developed in-house—should already be well understood. Each asset should have been selected, tuned, and integrated for a clear purpose. The PIR simply directs the right question to the most capable responder.

Step 3: Requirement Brokering—Executing the Intelligence Request

The final step is requirement brokering: the process by which the analyst delivers the PIR, along with necessary context, to the selected internal or external resource.

This is where the intelligence cycle becomes operational. The analyst isn't just matching a PIR to a system; they're tasking a team, tool, or vendor with executing a real collection or analytical task. This includes

- Providing background context
- Setting deadlines
- Clarifying output format (e.g., indicators, narrative report, scoring)
- Ensuring relevance to the original business need

Good brokering is both technical and interpersonal. Internally, it means aligning with SOC, IR, or fraud teams. Externally, it means managing vendor SLAs or expectations.

CHAPTER 5   UNDERSTANDING THE BUSINESS

IRM Process Diagram

Figure 5-1 is a visual representation of the three-step Information Requirement Management (IRM) process:

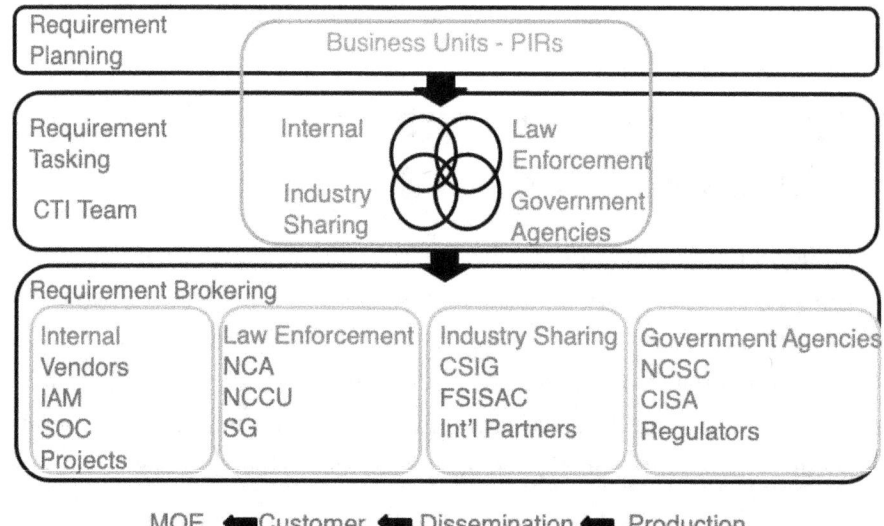

Figure 5-1. The Information Requirement Management (IRM) process

This diagram illustrates how intelligence requirements move from business units (top) through the CTI team (middle), and are finally brokered to the most suitable internal or external asset (bottom). It shows the structured flow from planning to tasking to brokering, including the categories of stakeholders involved—such as internal vendors, law enforcement, industry sharing groups, and government agencies.

The horizontal bands at the bottom—Production, Dissemination, Customer and Measure of Effect—indicate the alignment between measurement, audience, delivery method, and output type. These help ensure that CTI not only collects intelligence, but also delivers it in a format and at a level that is meaningful for business risk and decision-making.

Together, these three steps—Requirement Planning, Requirement Tasking, and Requirement Brokering—form the backbone of Information Requirement Management (IRM). This process ensures that intelligence isn't driven by tools or alerts but by a clear, stakeholder-aligned understanding of what the business needs to know to operate safely and confidently.

This is what it means to be intelligence-led.

The Art of Predictive Posturing

Horizon scanning involves meticulous observation of the cyber environment to anticipate and mitigate potential threats before they materialize. It requires a comprehensive understanding of emerging trends, technologies, threat actors, and attack methodologies. By staying informed of the evolving digital terrain and potential vulnerabilities, a cybersecurity analyst can identify indicators of impending threats.

Learning from Others' Encounters

A significant aspect of horizon scanning is learning from the experiences of others within the industry or sector. When a peer organization suffers an attack, this incident serves as a valuable case study. Being responsive to such an attack—studying it, understanding how it was carried out, and evaluating its impact—provides crucial insights that can strengthen your own cyber defenses.

Preemptive Control Enhancements

In response to intelligence gleaned from horizon scanning, preemptive control enhancements are critical. They involve adjusting and upgrading security measures in light of new information. This might include patching newly discovered vulnerabilities, implementing additional layers of security, or educating employees about novel phishing techniques. Such enhancements are not merely reactive adjustments to known threats but proactive preparations for potential future attacks, inferred from the broader context of what is happening to others in the digital ecosystem.

The Virtue of Preparing for the "What Ifs"

Preemptive preparation requires a certain level of creativity and strategic forecasting. It means asking "what if" and preparing for scenarios that have not yet, and may never, occur. This preparation positions a business to not only withstand known threats but to also be resilient against unknown challenges. It means shifting from a mindset of recovery—bouncing back after a blow—to one of resilience—being structured in such a way that even unforeseen blows can be absorbed.

The Synthesis of Response and Prediction

In the end, horizon scanning synthesizes responsive action with predictive analytics. It underlines the adage that the best defense is a good offense, and in the world of cybersecurity, offense is not about striking back but about being steps ahead. By adopting an "over the horizon" approach, a business can transform cybersecurity from a narrative of survival into a tale of strategic mastery.

In the ever-shifting landscape of cybersecurity, horizon scanning is a principle that transcends mere vigilance—it represents a proactive and forward-thinking stance. Having an "over the horizon" focus is a commitment to being predictive rather than merely responsive.

CHAPTER 5   UNDERSTANDING THE BUSINESS

Threat Postulation

Discuss the process of hypothesizing potential threats based on known data and intelligence, a critical step in proactive cyber defense.

In the world of cybersecurity, the concept of threat intelligence might seem straightforward when discussed within the siloed confines of an intelligence department. However, the true challenge arises when one attempts to translate this intelligence into meaningful insights for the specific areas of the business it might impact. Too often, there exists a chasm between the intelligence gathered and its practical application within the operational units of a company.

The disconnection is not necessarily due to inexperience; it may stem more profoundly from a lack of security culture within the organization. Indeed, as the maxim goes, "only leadership can change the culture." Intelligence reaches its zenith of effectiveness not when hoarded at the executive level but when it is disseminated among the operational teams, enabling them to integrate this knowledge into the security considerations of their function from the very beginning—the design phase.

To bridge the gap, it is imperative to initiate dialogue with business units. It involves sitting with them, discussing the threats, and more importantly, asking them to conceptualize what those threats signify for their specific operations. This exercise can require a gentle, yet firm nudge, as operational teams might not initially see the relevance or have the inclination to engage with abstract threats. However, the benefits of such an engagement are manifold. By understanding the direct implications of a threat, teams can bolster the effectiveness of security controls with a level of precision and customization that generic measures cannot achieve.

Let's consider a simple military anecdote to illustrate this point. When assessing threats to the UK, Home Grown Islamic Extremist terrorism was identified as a primary concern. To the Royal Air Force (RAF), this broad categorization needed to be distilled into a specific scenario that could inform actionable defense strategies. With the threat postulated as

45

CHAPTER 5   UNDERSTANDING THE BUSINESS

a potential grenade attack by terrorists on a critical RAF base, actionable measures could be implemented: solidifying and elevating the perimeter fence, relocating the Quick Response Force (QRF), and enhancing surveillance at strategic points. Without the RAF's expert input, the generic threat would not have been translated into such targeted defense improvements.

Similarly, in the cyber realm, it is vitally important to delve into the specifics. An organization may benefit from hiring a consultant or embedding a Cyber Threat Intelligence (CTI) analyst within the business unit itself. This level of integration ensures that threat intelligence is not just a report that gathers dust on a shelf but a dynamic, living guide that informs daily operations and strategic defense planning.

Conclusion

The key is to foster a security-centric culture, led from the top, but implemented at all levels. Only then can the full potential of threat intelligence be harnessed to fortify an organization's cyber defenses with the granularity and foresight that the modern digital battlefield demands.

CHAPTER 6

Create the Vectors: Vector First—Actor Second

All the business of war, and indeed all the business of life, is to endeavour to find out what you don't know from what you do.

—The Duke of Wellington

This chapter introduces the methodology of focusing on the nature of the threat itself before considering who might be behind it, emphasizing the importance of understanding attack methods over attribution.

In the evolving field of CTI, a long-standing debate continues: should efforts prioritize tracking specific threat actors, or should the focus shift to the tactics, techniques, and procedures (TTPs) they use? This book firmly supports the latter approach. Effective threat management stems not from knowing *who* is behind an attack but from understanding *how* they operate.

The MITRE ATT&CK framework reinforces this concept by offering a structured, globally recognized taxonomy of adversary behaviors. Take phishing, for instance. Within the ATT&CK matrix, phishing is categorized under Initial Access—the first phase in an attack chain. By detecting and mitigating this early-stage technique, organizations can potentially disrupt over 50% of subsequent attack techniques that would otherwise unfold along the adversary's path.[1]

This illustrates a key principle: focusing on early-stage TTPs can have an outsized impact on defense. Understanding and preemptively countering the method—not just the actor—provides a more agile, scalable, and preventative approach to cybersecurity.

The Primacy of TTPs

While comprehending a threat actor's capabilities and intentions holds value, such information is more effectively utilized when interpreted through the lenses of potential impact and likelihood of targeting one's business. Concentrating on TTPs allows security teams to adapt defenses to a wide range of attacks, regardless of the adversary behind them. It equips organizations with the resilience to withstand known threats and the agility to respond to new ones.

The Challenge of Attribution

While not dismissing the relevance of attribution, this text posits that it must not overshadow the primary objective: gaining intimate knowledge of TTPs. Attribution can be an intricate, time-consuming process often mired in uncertainty. It serves a secondary role, one that potentially complements—but does not eclipse—the practical defenses shaped around known TTPs.

---

[1] Cisco Talos Incident Response, "IR Trends Q1 2025: Phishing soars as identity-based attacks persist" (28th Apr 2025): "Threat actors used phishing to achieve initial access in 50% of engagements, a notable increase from less than 10% last quarter." https://blog.talosintelligence.com/ir-trends-q1-2025/

Learning from Experience

Experience often serves as the harshest teacher. A board member might challenge the relevance of being briefed about a specific version of ransomware, prompting the inevitable question, "So what?" The implication here is not a dismissal of the threat but a call for actionable intelligence—how does it affect us, and what can we do about it?

Similarly, an overemphasis on tracking a select list of known threat actors can result in a critical oversight: failing to detect emerging players who might target peer organizations. Such blind spots can lead to unanticipated breaches, illustrating the necessity of a method-centric approach.

The "Big 5" Threat Vectors

The methods utilized by adversaries are categorized into five primary threat vectors: Phishing, Malware, DDoS (Distributed Denial of Service), Hacking, and Insider threats. By dissecting these vectors, security teams can devise strategies that address the broadest spectrum of cyber threats. Each vector encapsulates a range of TTPs which, when understood and anticipated, form the cornerstone of a proactive cyber defense strategy.

Phishing

Phishing is a type of social engineering attack used to steal user data, including login credentials and financial information. It typically involves attackers masquerading as trusted entities in emails, instant messages, or text messages to trick recipients into clicking malicious links or downloading infected attachments. While this remains true, the phishing landscape has evolved.

CHAPTER 6 CREATE THE VECTORS: VECTOR FIRST—ACTOR SECOND

Modern phishing attacks are increasingly sophisticated and targeted. One key evolution is Business Email Compromise[2] (BEC)—where attackers compromise or spoof legitimate business accounts to defraud employees, partners, or customers. These attacks are often text-based, with no malware or malicious links, making them harder to detect by traditional means.

Attackers also increasingly use legitimate URLs that redirect to credential harvesting pages or drop malware hosted on reputable platforms.[3] Attachments, once crude and easily detectable, now frequently use obfuscation or macros to deliver initial access malware or droppers.

A fundamental CTI message is this: unsolicited emails should always be treated with caution. Regardless of content, source, or presentation, phishing emails exploit trust—and trust can be engineered.

Effective phishing intelligence reporting must remain simple, consistent, and impactful. It should answer

- How many malicious emails were received?
- How many were blocked automatically?
- How many were clicked?
- What was the content and format?
- Was malware involved? What kind?
- Where did it direct the user?

---

[2] FBI Internet Crime Complaint Center (IC3), 2024 Internet Crime Report (23rd Apr 2025) p. 19: Business Email Compromise accounted for $2.77 billion in reported losses during 2024, the single costliest crime category tracked by IC3. https://www.fbi.gov/news/press-releases/fbi-releases-annual-internet-crime-report

[3] Proofpoint Threat Research, "Stopping Phishing Attacks that Pivot from Email to SMS" (Blog, 16th May 2025): "Over the past three years there has been a 119% increase in URL threats delivered by email." https://www.proofpoint.com/au/blog/email-and-cloud-threats/stopping-phishing-email-to-sms

- Which parts of the business were targeted?
- Has this type of attack been seen across the wider industry?

This clarity not only aids decision-making but also supports awareness campaigns and board-level reporting. And it is crucial to remember—the absence of impact does not mean the absence of threat.

Boards and risk committees may become complacent if phishing hasn't caused a major breach—yet. But the minute phishing protections are reduced or removed, adversaries will exploit the gap. Phishing remains one of the most effective and low-cost ways for attackers to gain access, and its success is only a click away.

Malware

Malware, short for malicious software, refers to any software intentionally designed to cause damage to a computer, server, client, or network. While traditional definitions list types like viruses, worms, trojans, ransomware, and spyware, modern CTI must go far beyond naming conventions.

In today's threat landscape, malware is no longer the preserve of elite threat actors. It has been commoditized and weaponized to the point where even semi-skilled cybercriminals or hacktivists can launch attacks using "malware-as-a-service" (MaaS) platforms. These platforms offer a near plug-and-play experience, often via websites designed to build, configure, and deploy malware in exchange for cryptocurrency payments. It's a jukebox-style attack model: insert your fee, select your malware features, and press play.

CHAPTER 6   CREATE THE VECTORS: VECTOR FIRST—ACTOR SECOND

This lowers the barrier to entry dramatically and has led to a significant proliferation of malware variants, many of which are built on common codebases, but customized with new payloads or evasion techniques.[4]

Additionally, understanding malware requires contextual classification:

- **Initial Access Malware**: Often delivered via phishing or exploit kits, designed solely to gain a foothold.

- **Droppers**: Lightweight programs used to download or install secondary malware after initial access is established.

- **Second-Stage Malware**: Often more sophisticated, these carry out the primary payload—such as data exfiltration, lateral movement, or ransomware encryption.

An intelligence-led view must recognize that malware is part of a life cycle, not a stand-alone threat. The analyst must understand where the malware fits in the kill chain, what its deployment says about the adversary's intent, and what its functionality implies for organizational risk.

Ransomware: A Weaponized Evolution of Malware

Ransomware represents one of the most evolved and disruptive forms of malware, earning its place as a top-tier threat under the broader malware

---

[4] Control D, "100 Malware Statistics & Trends (2023–2025)" (4th Feb 2025): "In 2024, malware-as-a-service offerings are expected to expand by 30% on the dark web, fueling widespread commoditization." https://controld.com/blog/malware-statistics-trends/

vector. While it shares technical roots with traditional malicious software, ransomware has diverged through commercialization, operational sophistication, and strategic impact—transforming from a blunt cyber weapon into a finely tuned extortion ecosystem.

The Growth and Proliferation of Ransomware

Ransomware has grown not just in frequency but in maturity. What began as indiscriminate, opportunistic attacks against individual users has evolved into highly targeted campaigns against businesses, governments, and critical national infrastructure. This evolution has been fueled by the rise of Ransomware-as-a-Service (RaaS)—a business model where developers lease ransomware payloads to affiliates, who then carry out attacks in exchange for a revenue share.

This service-based model has commoditized ransomware. Affiliates can select from a menu of ransomware variants, choose encryption methods, customize ransom notes, and even access victim negotiation support and payment processing via TOR-based portals.

Ransomware Methodology: From Access to Encryption

A typical ransomware campaign unfolds as follows:

1. **Initial Access**: Often achieved through phishing, brute-force attacks on RDP (Remote Desktop Protocol), or exploiting known vulnerabilities.

2. **Establishing Persistence**: Using tools like Cobalt Strike or built-in OS features to maintain access.

3. **Credential Harvesting**: Targeting domain admins to escalate privileges.

4. **Lateral Movement**: Using legitimate tools like PsExec, PowerShell, or remote access protocols to spread within the environment.

5. **Payload Delivery**: Deployment of the ransomware binary, often after disabling antivirus or backup services.

6. **Encryption and Exfiltration**: Files are encrypted, and increasingly, data is exfiltrated before encryption to enable double or triple extortion.

7. **Extortion**: Victims are threatened with public exposure or regulatory reporting if payment is not made.

This structured methodology has made ransom**ware more coordinated and catastrophic than ever.**

What Makes Ransomware Unique

- **Financially Motivated and Organized**: Unlike other malware, ransomware is not about espionage or disruption—it's about profit.

- **Double and Triple Extortion**: Beyond encryption, threat actors now threaten to leak data or notify regulators, multiplying pressure.[5]

---

[5] Control D, "100 Malware Statistics & Trends (2023–2025)" (4th Feb 2025): "Double-extortion ransomware accounted for 81% of incidents in 2023; triple extortion reached 14%." https://controld.com/blog/malware-statistics-trends/

- **Human-Operated Attacks:** Many modern ransomware groups rely on human[6] operators to plan and tailor attacks to the victim, bypassing automated detection.
- **Short Dwell Time, Long Consequence**: The time between intrusion and encryption[7] is often short, but the recovery and business impact can be prolonged.

Detecting Ransomware

Detection is increasingly difficult due to the use of

- Fileless malware
- Legitimate administrative tools
- Obfuscation and encryption techniques

Tools like EDR/XDR, behavior-based anomaly detection, and deception technologies (honeypots, sandboxing) are essential.

Key Indicators of Ransomware Operations Include

- Unusual use of legitimate tools (e.g., PowerShell, VSSAdmin)
- Sudden spikes in file renaming or encryption patterns
- Communication with known C2 infrastructure or TOR domains
- Disabling of antivirus or backup systems

---

[6] Verizon DBIR 2024 shows 68% of breaches involve the human element https://www.verizon.com/business/resources/reports/dbir/

[7] Mandiant, M-Trends 2024 (23rd Apr 2024) p. 4: Global median dwell time fell to 10 days in 2023, down from 16 days in 2022. https://cloud.google.com/blog/topics/threat-intelligence/m-trends-2024

CHAPTER 6   CREATE THE VECTORS: VECTOR FIRST—ACTOR SECOND

Why Ransomware Matters to CTI Teams

Ransomware is not just a technical event—it's a business risk event. It impacts brand trust, regulatory exposure, legal liability, and operational continuity. CTI teams must

- Monitor ransomware affiliate activity on dark web forums.
- Track emerging RaaS variants and TTPs.
- Collect Indicators of Compromise (IOCs) for detection.
- Understand which business units are at greatest risk.
- Align with backup, DR, legal, and comms teams.

Key PIRs for Ransomware Intelligence

1. What new RaaS variants are being advertised or traded?
2. Are any affiliates discussing targeting our sector or region?
3. Have new vulnerabilities or exploits been weaponized by ransomware groups?
4. What TTPs are most associated with initial access in current ransomware attacks?
5. Have ransomware indicators been detected in our environment or supply chain?
6. Which ransomware groups are currently most active and what are their negotiation tactics?

Ransomware represents the commercial apex of the malware threat vector. It is profitable, persistent, and increasingly professional. By treating ransomware not just as malware but as an **ecosystem**, CTI teams can shift

CHAPTER 6   CREATE THE VECTORS: VECTOR FIRST—ACTOR SECOND

from reactive response to strategic anticipation—knowing not just what has happened but who might be next, how, and why.

Monitoring ransomware is not optional. It's an essential function of a mature CTI capability.

DDoS (Distributed Denial of Service)

DDoS Attacks involve a network of compromised computers, known as a "botnet," which is used to flood a website with fake traffic, overwhelming the site's capacity to handle multiple requests. This causes the site to slow down significantly or crash altogether,[8] denying service to legitimate users trying to access the website.

The threat posed by DDoS attacks has continued to progressively be a concern for all organizations. Over the past eight years, most large multinational institutions have experienced their first DDoS attack that impacted the organization. Increasing in frequency, size and pace and sophistication, the attacks using Mirai botnet marked a new era of mega DDoS attacks,[9] leveraging compromised IoT devices to undertake malicious activity. It asks the question—are there parts of the Internet that could become unavailable? What services would be affected? Do we have a contingency plan? Is your Internet Service Provider providing suitable protection?

---

[8] NETSCOUT, DDoS Threat Intelligence Report, 2H 2024: recorded 8.9 million attacks worldwide (↑ 12.8% YoY) with a peak bandwidth assault of 995 Gbps. https://www.netscout.com/threatreport/

[9] Cloudflare Research, "Largest-ever DDoS attack stopped — Mirai variant in play" (19th Jun 2025): single burst exceeded 7.3 terabits per second (Tbps), sourced from 122k IoT devices running Mirai code. https://blog.cloudflare.com/defending-the-internet-how-cloudflare-blocked-a-monumental-7-3-tbps-ddos/

CHAPTER 6   CREATE THE VECTORS: VECTOR FIRST—ACTOR SECOND

Hacking

Hacking refers to unauthorized intrusion into a device or network. The person engaged in hacking activities is known as a hacker. This person may alter system or security features to accomplish a goal that differs from the original purpose of the system. Hacking can be used to steal information, damage data, or disrupt service.

It is increasingly likely that organizations that rely on third party software and SaaS solutions will be significantly impacted by a directly targeted attack on software vulnerabilities and zero days.[10] With software being released and updated more frequently than ever, the requirement to maintain awareness of vulnerabilities and speed of patching has never been more important. The tactic of threat actors rushing to code an exploit for a recent vulnerability is being employed by highly motivated and capable threat actors, which highlights the need for rapid and agile patching.

Insider

An **Insider Threat** is a security risk that originates within the targeted organization. It involves an individual or group of individuals who have inside information concerning the organization's security practices, data, and computer systems. An insider threat does not always mean someone of malicious intent but could also be a well-meaning employee who

---

[10] Rapid7, 2024 Attack Intelligence Report (May 2024): 60% of vulnerabilities in network/security appliances were exploited as zero-days; edge-device exploitation nearly doubled vs. 2023. https://www.rapid7.com/blog/post/2024/05/21/rapid7-releases-the-2024-attack-intelligence-report/

negligently handles data or falls victim to social engineering or phishing[11] schemes.

The **Insider Threat** encompasses a wide range of risks, including those that arise from employees' accidental or negligent actions that can compromise the security of an organization. This can occur through various means such as:

1. **Accidental Data Exposure**: An employee might unintentionally share sensitive information with unauthorized parties due to a lack of understanding of security protocols or simple human error.

2. **Misdelivery of Information**: Sending sensitive emails to the wrong recipient or misplacing documents can lead to data breaches.

3. **Insecure Use of Technology**: Employees, using unsecured networks to access corporate resources, or failing to follow security best practices when using their devices, can inadvertently create entry points for attackers.

4. **Poor Password Hygiene**: Using weak passwords or reusing passwords across multiple services can inadvertently compromise security.

Given the commonality of such incidents, it is crucial for security controls to be designed not only to guard against malicious insiders but also to mitigate the risks posed by non-malicious actions.[12] This could involve implementing strict data access controls, conducting regular

---

[11] Verizon DBIR 2024: 20% report, 11% both click & report https://www.verizon.com/business/resources/reports/dbir/

[12] Ponemon Institute, 2025 Cost of Insider Threats Global Report: average direct cost per insider incident $648k; breaches contained in > 90 days averaged $18.7 M, vs. $10.6 M when contained in ≤ 30 days. https://ponemon.dtexsystems.com/

training on security awareness, employing advanced encryption for data at rest and in transit, and using monitoring tools to detect and respond to unusual activity that could indicate a potential security lapse. The goal is to create a security infrastructure that is as forgiving of human error as it is resilient to deliberate sabotage.

The Big 5—Understanding and Reporting Threat Vectors

In the field of CTI, identifying and categorizing cyber threats helps structure intelligence efforts, streamline communication with stakeholders, and prioritize defenses. One of the most effective models for this is focusing on what this book refers to as "The Big 5" threat vectors: Malware, Phishing, DDoS, Insider, and Hacking.

Each of these vectors represents a primary method by which threat actors compromise, disrupt, or exploit an organization.[13] Understanding the characteristics, methods, impacts, and mitigation strategies associated with each vector provides a foundational framework for intelligence teams, security leaders, and business executives alike.

Why the Big 5 Matters

The Big 5 is not just a conceptual model—it's a practical tool for organizing and delivering CTI. It

- Provides a shared language across technical and non-technical teams
- Helps guide intelligence requirements and vendor selection

---

[13] ENISA, Threat Landscape 2024 p. 4: of seven prime threats analyzed, Threats-against-availability (DDoS) ranked #1, ransomware/malware #2, and data threats #3, underscoring that these vectors are the primary paths for compromise. https://www.enisa.europa.eu/publications/enisa-threat-landscape-2024

CHAPTER 6   CREATE THE VECTORS: VECTOR FIRST—ACTOR SECOND

- Supports vulnerability and threat assessments
- Enables streamlined reporting

More importantly, it allows organizations to align their defenses with realistic, recurring threats based on observed adversary behaviors.[14]

Single-Page Reporting with the Big 5 Table

Table 6-1 is a one-page visualization that serves as a highly effective CTI reporting tool. It captures the essential characteristics of each threat vector—key issues, common methods, potential impacts, current controls, and future focus areas:

Table 6-1. *CTI Single-Page Reporting*

Threat Considerations	Event	Method Used	Impact	Key Mitigating Control	Future Focus
Malware	WannaCry NotPetya, Ransomware	Network attack, Phishing	Extensive operational disruption and losses	Vulnerability Management, User Education and SA	Patch Management & Threat Monitoring, Ed & SA
Phishing	Significant spikes? New vectors (social media etc.)	Email, Voicecall, SMS, social media	Customer and bank losses	Security Awareness, Phishlabs	Security Awareness SMS Reporting Partnership Working, HVP
DDoS	Strongest level of attack seen 1.7TB	Hijacked devices forming BotNets, IoT Exploiting Applications.	Service Disruption, Extortion	DDoS mitigation (technical) service, Intelligence Sharing	Resilience and mitigation techniques
Insider	General theme - accidental or malicious action. SWIFT	Email, print, devices and web	Loss of confidential data. Blackmail	Anomaly detection Data loss prevention tools. Security culture	Security awareness & enhancing data protection. JML
Hacking	Leak of exploits used by NSA. Cyber Cold War.	Network attack – targeting unpatched systems	Compromised networks and confidential data.	Vulnerability Management, Pen Test/Red Teaming	Vulnerability Management & Network intrusion controls, Pen Test update

---

[14] NETSCOUT, DDoS Threat Intelligence Report — Issue 14 (2H 2024): logged 16.8M attacks worldwide (↑ 12.75% vs. 1H 2024) with a record 500 Gbps peak flood, illustrating the "recurring" nature of high-impact vectors. https://www.netscout.com/resources/latest-resources/threat-intelligence-report-issue-14-findings-from-2h-2024

CHAPTER 6   CREATE THE VECTORS: VECTOR FIRST—ACTOR SECOND

How to Use This Table

- CTI Teams can use this table to communicate current threat trends with clarity.

- Security Operations can align detection and response activities to known methods.

- Executives and Risk Managers can quickly grasp where risk lies and where investment is needed.

The table also encourages cross-functional awareness—bringing together teams focused on phishing awareness, patch management, third-party risk, and more. It highlights how each vector is distinct yet interconnected in the broader security landscape.[15]

In mature CTI programs, this model becomes more than a static chart—it evolves into a live, interactive dashboard, with links to incident data, intelligence reports, and risk ratings per vector.

By standardizing how threats are visualized and discussed, the Big 5 framework simplifies complexity and ensures alignment across the organization.

The Analyst's Role in Impact and Understanding

This chapter makes a clear case for prioritizing the study and mitigation of TTPs above all else. It encourages organizations to develop a nuanced understanding of the various threat vectors and to tailor their defense

---

[15] Ponemon Institute, 2025 Cost of Insider Threats Global Report: average annual cost per organization $17.4 M; incidents contained in > 91 days averaged $18.7 M vs $10.6 M when contained ≤ 30 days—evidence that insider risk is both common and costly. https://ponemon.dtexsystems.com/

mechanisms accordingly. In doing so, it is possible to forge a security posture that is not only robust and comprehensive, but also nimble and anticipatory—qualities essential in the ever-evolving battleground of cybersecurity.

Yet knowing the threat is only part of the responsibility. The value of CTI is not just in identifying threats but in understanding their potential impact. This is where the art of intelligence—and the insight of the analyst—truly shines.

To illustrate this, consider Figure 6-1.

Figure 6-1. *Understanding the adversary*

This picture symbolizes the role of the intelligence analyst. The snake is venomous. The analyst knows this—not only through label or appearance, but through study of its behavior, venom type, historical bites, and known antidotes. The question is: if bitten, do you cut off the finger or the whole arm to save the body?

This analogy underscores several key lessons:

- **Understanding the adversary matters**: Motivation, region, tactics, and evolution all play a role.

- **Impact matters as much as identification**: Knowing what malware is used is not enough—what it can do and where it strikes must be understood.

- **Threats evolve**: You may have already mitigated "this" snake, but what happens when it sheds its skin or strikes differently?

- **Controls are not permanent**: Defense must adapt to changes in threat behavior. What was mitigated yesterday may be vulnerable today.

Intelligence is not a static product—it is a living process. The analyst must constantly reassess not just the existence of threats but their implications, movement, and consequences. It is only with this complete understanding of threat vector and impact that security decisions can be made confidently. Having an expert who instantly recognizes the threat saves time and potentially the network.

Overlapping Vectors

The threat vectors can intersect and overlap or interact, which is expected when understanding threat complexity.

The concept of focusing on the Big 5 cyber threat vectors—Phishing, Malware, DDoS, Hacking, and Insider—highlights the interconnected nature of cyber threats. When we estimate these threats holistically rather than as isolated incidents, the overlaps become apparent and significant. Such a comprehensive approach underscores the complexity of cybersecurity and the necessity for integrated defensive strategies.

For example, consider a typical cyberattack scenario:

- **Phishing**: The attack often begins with a phishing email, which appears to be from a legitimate source. This is a critical initial access strategy used by attackers.

- **Malware**: The phishing email may contain malicious attachments or links. When clicked by an unsuspecting victim, these links can lead to the installation of malware.

- **Execution and Propagation**: Once the malware is installed, it can perform a variety of functions, from stealing data to encrypting files for ransom, or even using the infected machine as a launch pad for further attacks within the network.

- **Facilitating Further Attacks**: The compromised system may also provide the necessary credentials or network access to facilitate further hacking attempts, either manually by the attackers or automatically by the malware.

- **Insider Facilitation**: In some cases, insider threats can also leverage the confusion during a malware infection to mask their activities or to assist in the spread of the malware, whether knowingly or unknowingly.

This overlap of vectors in a single attack illustrates why a siloed approach to cybersecurity can be less effective. Instead, understanding how these vectors interplay can help in crafting more resilient defenses. For instance

- **Integrated Security Solutions**: Employing solutions that can detect and respond to multiple types of threats—like unified threat management (UTM) systems—can be more effective than using separate tools for each type of threat.

- **Employee Training**: Comprehensive security training for employees can help mitigate the risks not only of phishing but also of insider threats, as well-trained employees are more likely to recognize and avoid suspicious links and attachments.

- **Layered Defense**: Implementing a layered defense strategy[16] that includes network segmentation, endpoint protection, and proactive monitoring can help prevent the propagation of an attack, even if the initial defenses are breached.

Thus, by viewing the threat landscape through a holistic lens, organizations can develop a more effective cybersecurity posture that addresses the complex and interwoven nature of modern cyber threats.

---

[16] IBM & Ponemon, Cost of a Data Breach Report 2024: the global average breach cost rose 10% to $4.88 M, and breaches involving stolen credentials lasted 292 days on average—demonstrating why layered, integrated defenses and rapid containment are essential. https://www.ibm.com/reports/data-breach

CHAPTER 7

Geopolitics

It is critical to analyze how international politics, relations, and events influence cyber threats and the security landscape.

Geopolitics is the study of the effects of geography, economics, demographics, and cultural factors on the politics and relations between states or regions. In today's complex and rapidly changing world, geopolitical events such as regional conflicts, political instability, and economic shifts have far-reaching impacts, affecting global markets, supply chains, and security.[1] With G7 nations[2] actively involved in state-sponsored cyber activities or leading efforts to combat national and international cyber threats, there is a heightened need for actionable intelligence. The interconnectedness brought about by global social media and instant news feeds has made executives and board members more

---

[1] World Economic Forum, Global Risks Report 2024 (10th Jan 2024) p. 9: "Geoeconomic confrontation and interstate conflict rank among the top 10 global risks over the next two years, with cascading impacts on energy, supply chains, and cyber-security." https://www.weforum.org/publications/global-risks-report-2024/

[2] G7 Foreign Ministers, "Addressing Global Challenges & Fostering Partnerships" (19th Apr 2024): "We will increase our cooperation against malicious cyber activities, including state-sponsored ones, and strengthen collective resilience." https://www.gov.uk/government/publications/g7-foreign-ministers-meeting-communiques-april-2024/g7-foreign-ministers-meeting-communique-capri-19-april-2024-addressing-global-challenges-fostering-partnerships

CHAPTER 7   GEOPOLITICS

informed and eager for insights on how these geopolitical events affect their businesses.

In this environment, CTI teams must understand and integrate geopolitical analysis into their reporting. Here are the top 10 best practices for handling geopolitical reporting within a CTI framework.

The top 10 best practices for a CTI team include

1. **Do Not Confuse Geopolitics with the Big 5 Cyber Threat Vectors.** The Big 5[3] cyber threat vectors—Phishing, Malware, Distributed Denial of Service (DDoS), Hacking, and Insider threats—remain core to threat analysis, but geopolitical factors can influence the likelihood and nature of these threats. When reporting, identify overlaps between specific regions and relevant threat vectors. For instance, a geopolitical conflict may increase the risk of state-sponsored hacking, targeting critical infrastructure.[4]

2. **Maintain a Cyber Context in Reporting.** Ensure all geopolitical reporting is framed within a cybersecurity context, or there's no reason to report it. The relevance to your organization's security posture should be clear, and reporting expectations should be set early. CTI teams are not news agencies or weather reporters; the focus should remain

---

[3] Verizon, 2024 Data Breach Investigations Report p. 49: among 30,458 incidents, Denial-of-Service accounted for > 50% of incidents while Social-Engineering (phishing/pretexting) figured in 36% and Malware in 27%, confirming the dominance of the "Big 5" vectors. https://www.verizon.com/business/resources/reports/dbir/

[4] CISA, Alert (30th Jun 2025): Warns CISA and Partners Urge Critical Infrastructure to Stay Vigilant in the Current Geopolitical Environment https://www.cisa.gov/news-events/alerts/2025/06/30/cisa-and-partners-urge-critical-infrastructure-stay-vigilant-current-geopolitical-environment

on the cyber risks and threats associated with geopolitical events.

3. **Select Vendors with Geopolitical Expertise.** Partner with vendors who offer specialized geopolitical intelligence services to enhance your collection efforts. Vendors with a strong understanding of regional dynamics and their implications for cyber threats can provide critical insights that general threat intelligence sources may not cover.

4. **Build Specific PIRs for Geopolitical Collection.** Prioritized Intelligence Requirements (PIRs) for geopolitical intelligence should be tailored to the regions and issues of interest. This ensures that intelligence gathering efforts are focused and relevant, allowing for targeted analysis of how geopolitical events might influence the cyber threat landscape.

5. **Monitor Cyber Activity in Hybrid Conflict Environments.** When covering regions involved in conflicts, be aware of hybrid warfare tactics,[5] which may combine kinetic (physical) and non-kinetic (cyber) operations. Cyber activities can serve as a precursor to, or follow-up from, physical military actions. Monitor for signs of cyber activity that may disrupt critical infrastructure or target businesses with operations in affected regions.

---

[5] Lawfare, "Cyber Conflict and Subversion in the Russia-Ukraine War" (11th Jun 2024): Details how Russian hacking groups used wiper malware and satellite-modem sabotage as part of a hybrid warfare campaign coordinated with kinetic. https://www.lawfaremedia.org/article/cyber-conflict-in-the-russia-ukraine-war

CHAPTER 7   GEOPOLITICS

6. **Understand the Supply Chain Risks and Business Footprint in Affected Regions.** Assess the significance of the region for the organization's supply chain and evaluate potential vulnerabilities.[6] Consider the importance of the goods and services sourced from the region, the potential risks posed by geopolitical instability, and how regional dynamics might impact the company's local operations, offices, data centers, and service providers.

7. **Be Sensitive to Regional Colleagues.** Geopolitical conflicts may directly impact colleagues who are from or currently living in the regions being reported on. Sensitivity is required in reporting to avoid unnecessary distress or bias. Maintain an awareness of cultural nuances and the human element when assessing the impact of geopolitical events.

8. **Remain Culturally Aware and Unbiased.** Avoid letting personal or organizational biases influence analysis and assessments. Geopolitical reporting should be based on facts and data, not preconceived notions or political views. Cultural awareness and sensitivity in analysis are essential for producing balanced and accurate intelligence.

---

[6] ENISA, Threat Landscape 2023 (Oct 2023) Supply-Chain Attacks p. 86: Supply-chain intrusions "surpassed malware-based data breaches by 133%," with SolarWinds cited as a key example of cascading risk. https://www.enisa.europa.eu/publications/enisa-threat-landscape-2023

9. **Conclude Reports with a "So What?" to the Business.** Geopolitical events may appear to be grand in scale and strategic in nature, but CTI reporting should always answer the question, "So what does this mean for our business?" Clearly explain the implications for the organization, whether it's a potential increase in cyber threats, disruption to operations, or changes in regulatory risks.

10. **Work Collaboratively with Law Enforcement, Government Agencies, and Intelligence Sharing Communities.** Engage with entities that focus on geopolitical intelligence, including law enforcement agencies, governmental bodies, and intelligence-sharing communities. Collaborative efforts can provide a more comprehensive view of the threat landscape and validate findings. Partners may also offer additional insights that are not accessible through standard intelligence sources.

Applying Geopolitical Intelligence to Cyber Threat Reporting

To effectively integrate geopolitical intelligence into cyber threat reporting, CTI teams should

- **Map out the geographic and political landscapes** affecting the business. Understand how different regions are interconnected and how changes in one area can influence cyber risks in another.

- **Identify the most relevant threat vectors** in the context of geopolitical events. If a state-sponsored actor is targeting critical infrastructure, for instance, there may be a higher likelihood of specific types of cyberattacks, such as DDoS or ransomware.

- **Leverage threat intelligence feeds** that specialize in geopolitical data. These feeds can provide early warnings about potential state-sponsored cyber activities, sanctions, or regulatory changes that may impact operations.

Conclusion

Geopolitical events have far-reaching implications, and their effects can extend to cybersecurity. By following these best practices, CTI teams can produce meaningful intelligence that helps organizations navigate an increasingly uncertain world. Geopolitical reporting is not about providing general news; it's about assessing how events will impact the business's security and providing actionable recommendations to mitigate risks.

CHAPTER 8

Fraud

Cyber fraud is one of the most pressing threats facing organizations today, especially in the financial sector.[1] Defined as the intentional deception or manipulation of digital systems to unlawfully acquire financial or personal information, cyber fraud exploits digital and online platforms, often targeting vulnerabilities in both human behavior and digital security. Unlike traditional fraud, cyber fraud leverages technology to amplify the scale and sophistication of attacks, resulting in significant financial and reputational risks.[2]

In the context of cyber threat intelligence, cyber fraud encompasses various interconnected categories, including cyber-enabled fraud, anti-fraud operations, cybercrime, and financial crime teams. Cyber Threat Intelligence (CTI) teams must collaborate with these specialized groups to share insights and enhance detection, mitigation, and response strategies for cyber fraud. Below, we explore cyber fraud definitions, how it manifests, and best practices to help organizations mitigate and manage its risks.

---

[1] LexisNexis Risk Solutions, True Cost of Fraud™ Study—Financial Services Edition (Press release, 24th Apr 2024): "Every dollar of fraud now costs North American financial institutions $4.41 in total outlay." https://risk.lexisnexis.com/global/en/about-us/press-room/press-release/20240424-tcof-financial-services-lending

[2] UK Finance, Annual Fraud Report 2024 (3rd Jun 2024) p. 10: UK banks and card issuers still lost £1.17 billion to fraud in 2023 despite a 3% year-over-year decline. https://www.ukfinance.org.uk/policy-and-guidance/reports-and-publications/annual-fraud-report-2024

CHAPTER 8   FRAUD

Key Types of Cyber Fraud

1. **Cyber-Enabled Fraud:** Cyber-enabled fraud refers to traditional fraud that has adapted to the digital landscape. Tactics such as phishing, spoofing, and social engineering take advantage of online channels to deceive users into revealing personal information, bank account details, and access credentials.

2. **Cyber Crime and Financial Crime Teams:** These teams often collaborate to investigate incidents that fall at the intersection of cybersecurity and finance, including unauthorized account access, fraudulent transactions, and data breaches. For CTI teams, working closely with these teams is vital to gaining context, sharing intelligence, and developing holistic security solutions.

3. **Internal and External Fraud Cases:** Cyber fraud can impact both external customers and internal employees. Externally, cyber fraud schemes like online banking theft and credit card fraud target account holders directly, often starting with the victim unwittingly providing personal information, logins, or passwords. Internally, employees may be targeted through social engineering, phishing emails, and spoofed requests to exploit their role within the organization.

4. **Evolving Attack Methods:** Phishing emails remain the most common tactic in cyber fraud,[3] serving as a vehicle to obtain sensitive information. However, the threat landscape has evolved with the rise of deepfake campaigns and phishing schemes involving document signing platforms like DocuSign.[4] These tactics exploit the familiarity and trust associated with these platforms, making detection and prevention more challenging.

Ten Best Practices for Combating Cyber Fraud

1. **Collaborate Closely with Internal Anti-Fraud Teams.** Foster a strong relationship with anti-fraud teams within the organization. Sharing intelligence and working together can uncover valuable insights into fraud trends, tactics, and vulnerabilities, enabling more effective and cohesive defense strategies.

2. **Define Cyber Fraud for the Organization.** Establish a clear and accessible definition of cyber fraud that resonates across departments.

---

[3] Verizon, 2025 Data Breach Investigations Report (23rd Apr 2025) p. 46: Phishing and Pretexting are still the main techniques leveraged to con employees. https://www.verizon.com/business/resources/reports/dbir/

[4] DocuSign Trust Center, Phishing Campaign Alert (6th Nov 2024): Advisory notes abuse of DocuSign APIs to send convincing fake invoices and deposit requests. https://www.docusign.com/trust/alerts/alert-phishing-campaign-observed-november-6-2024

CHAPTER 8   FRAUD

Standardized definitions help align anti-fraud, CTI, and cybersecurity teams on the organization's priorities and streamline the implementation of prevention and mitigation tools.

3. **Create PIRs Focused on Fraud as a Key Intelligence Theme.** Prioritized Intelligence Requirements (PIRs) specifically targeting fraud themes guide intelligence collection, helping CTI teams stay vigilant to evolving fraud tactics. This allows the organization to remain proactive in its approach to identifying and mitigating potential fraud threats.

4. **Gain Access to Online Banking and Credit Card Fraud Data.** Secure access to key fraud data related to online banking and credit card activity,[5] as these areas are frequent targets. Establishing protocols to access and analyze fraud data, while safeguarding customer identifiable information, allows CTI teams to spot emerging trends and threats.

---

[5] FBI, Internet Crime Complaint Center (IC3)—2024 Annual Report (23rd Apr 2025) p. 4: IC3 logged 859,532 complaints and $16.6 B in losses; credit-card/check fraud alone accounted for $33.8 M in reported losses. https://www.fbi.gov/news/press-releases/fbi-releases-annual-internet-crime-report

CHAPTER 8   FRAUD

5. **Develop Detection Rules for Known TTPs.** Create detection rules for recognized Tactics, Techniques, and Procedures (TTPs) used in cyber fraud.[6] For example, setting up alerts for DocuSign-related phishing attempts can help identify suspicious patterns and respond before they escalate.

6. **Collaborate with Cyber Threat Awareness and Education Teams.** Work with awareness teams to integrate cyber fraud topics into employee training programs. This ensures the workforce is knowledgeable about common fraud tactics, such as phishing and social engineering, and reinforces a culture of vigilance and proactive security.

7. **Integrate Cyber Fraud into Regular Intelligence Reporting.** Make cyber fraud a recurring subject in CTI-reporting agendas. This ensures ongoing visibility and keeps cyber fraud top-of-mind for leadership, allowing them to make informed decisions on resource allocation and strategic initiatives.

8. **Collect Intelligence from Law Enforcement and External Agencies.** Engage with external sources like Action Fraud and other law enforcement agencies dedicated to combating cyber fraud. These sources provide valuable intelligence on new tactics, criminal networks, and fraud trends, enhancing internal awareness and response capabilities.

---

[6] iProov Threat Intelligence Report 2025 (7th Feb 2024): Deepfake face-swap attacks: In 2024, attack volumes surged by 300% compared to 2023. https://www.iproov.com/reports/threat-intelligence-report-2025-remote-identity-attack

9. **Collaborate with the Payments Team for Secure Transaction Methods.** Partner with the payments team to develop more secure methods for client transactions. Establishing robust security practices for money transfers helps reduce the organization's exposure to fraud risks and demonstrates commitment to protecting clients' financial assets.

10. **Assign a CTI Team Member to Work with the Anti-Fraud Team.** If resources allow, assign a dedicated CTI team member to collaborate directly with the anti-fraud team. This integration can facilitate real-time intelligence sharing, strengthen defenses, and ensure that anti-fraud and CTI teams remain aligned on strategic objectives.

Conclusion

Cyber fraud poses a complex and pervasive threat to organizations, especially within the financial sector. By establishing a clear understanding of cyber fraud and adopting best practices focused on collaboration, targeted intelligence, and proactive defenses, organizations can mitigate cyber fraud risks and strengthen their resilience. Through close integration of CTI and anti-fraud efforts, organizations can build a unified approach to addressing both internal and external fraud, protecting their assets and upholding trust with customers and stakeholders.

CHAPTER 9

Spheres of Influence

Explore the roles different nations and organizations play in the cyber domain, from state-sponsored groups to private sector influencers.

In Cyber Threat Intelligence (CTI), understanding the spheres of influence is crucial for assessing risks and making informed decisions.[1] Figure 9-1 visualizes the spheres—Business, Micro, and Macro—that represent different levels of influence on an organization, each with its unique set of factors. This chapter will explore how to identify and label the relevant influences within each sphere and how they affect the organization.

The Three Spheres of Influence

The spheres of influence can be visualized as concentric circles surrounding the business, with the Business environment at the center, followed by the larger Micro environment, and finally the widest Macro environment. Each sphere encompasses different types of influences that can affect the organization in varying degrees. Layering the spheres

---

[1] NIST, Special Publication 800-30 Rev. 1—Guide for Conducting Risk Assessments (Sep 2012) §2.3: Risk must be analyzed at three tiers—organization, mission/business process, and information system—to inform decision-makers. https://csrc.nist.gov/pubs/sp/800/30/r1/final

with cyber considerations assists in the understanding of what decisions are within the business gift, or understanding that the further out, the decreasing control the business has on the subject.[2]

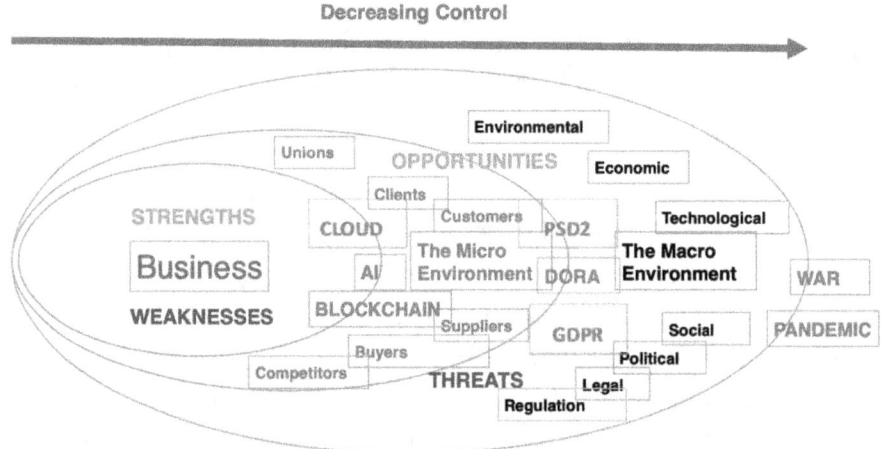

Figure 9-1. The Spheres of Influence

1. The Business Sphere (Innermost)

The Business sphere represents influences that are directly relevant to the organization and closely tied to its internal operations. These factors are typically within the organization's control and include elements specific to its functioning. Examples of influences in the Business sphere are

- **Audit and Compliance**: Internal checks, reviews, and adherence to internal policies.

- **Budget and Financial Resources**: Funding, financial management, and allocation of resources.

---

[2] Washington State University Libraries, "PESTEL Analysis" guide (27th Mar 2025): Describes the concentric-environment model (Political, Economic, Social, Technological, Environmental, Legal) for mapping internal vs. external control. https://libguides.libraries.wsu.edu/c.php?g=294263&p=4358409

- **Training and Skill Development**: Employee training programs and workforce skillsets.
- **Location and Facilities**: Geographical location of offices and operational sites.
- **Services and Products**: Offerings are directly controlled and managed by the business.

These influences are the most manageable, as they are internal and can be adjusted or optimized to meet business needs.

2. The Micro Sphere (Middle)

The Micro sphere encompasses factors that extend beyond the direct control of the business but still have a significant influence on its operations. These elements often involve interactions with external entities and cover a wider range of influences:

- **Competition**: Rival companies, market share, and industry trends
- **Technology**: Availability and development of technology that can impact operations
- **Regulation and Compliance**: External legal requirements and industry-specific regulations
- **Governance**: Corporate governance standards and best practices
- **Partnerships and Alliances**: Relationships with suppliers, clients, and other partners

While the business has some level of influence over these factors, they are shaped by interactions with external stakeholders and the wider industry environment.

CHAPTER 9   SPHERES OF INFLUENCE

3. The Macro Sphere (Outermost)

The Macro sphere covers the most far-reaching and external factors influencing the organization at a higher level. These influences extend beyond industry boundaries and impact society. They include

- **Religion and Culture**: Social norms, beliefs, and cultural practices that may affect business operations
- **Politics and Policy**: Government policies, political stability, and international relations
- **Environmental Factors**: Climate change, natural disasters, and environmental regulations
- **Global Economic Trends**: Economic cycles, inflation, and currency fluctuations

These factors are the least controllable by the business, as they are determined by global or regional dynamics and societal trends. While the organization can adapt to these influences, it cannot directly shape them.

Key observations when using the Spheres of Influence include

1. **Control Diminishes as Spheres Expand**: The further out the sphere extends, the lesser the degree of control the organization has over the factors within it. The Business sphere provides the most control, while the Macro sphere[3] offers the least. Recognizing this distinction helps prioritize efforts in areas where the business can make the most impact.

---

[3] Gartner, "6 Macro Factors That Will Reshape Business This Decade" (8th Feb 2023): Notes that macro forces are "largely outside any single enterprise's control yet decisive for strategy execution." https://www.gartner.com/en/articles/6-macro-factors-reshaping-business-this-decade

2. **Labeling Influences is Essential**: Identifying and labeling influences within each sphere is crucial for understanding their relevance to the business. This practice enables a structured approach to analyzing risks and opportunities. By categorizing factors under the correct sphere, the organization can better grasp their significance and address them accordingly.

3. **Adopting a Holistic Perspective**: Using the Spheres of Influence encourages a comprehensive view of the business environment. It allows the organization to evaluate internal factors while remaining aware of external risks and trends that could affect operations. This approach is essential for effective risk management[4] and strategic planning.

Applying the Spheres of Influence in Practice

To implement the spheres of influence framework effectively

- **Map out the factors** relevant to the business within each sphere. Start by listing internal factors in the Business sphere, followed by industry-specific influences in the Micro sphere, and then broader societal factors in the Macro sphere.

---

[4] Reuters/WEF, "Companies complacent about cyber-crime despite rising AI risk" (3rd Feb 2025): WEF's Global Cybersecurity Outlook stresses that boards must adopt a holistic, cross-layer approach to resilience because external macro factors intensify cyber risks. https://www.reuters.com/sustainability/sustainable-finance-reporting/esg-watch-companies-complacent-about-cybercrime-despite-rise-risk-ai-2025-02-03/

- **Prioritize efforts** based on the degree of control the organization has over each factor. Focus more on areas where the business can drive change (Business and Micro spheres) while staying informed about Macro influences.
- **Regularly review and update** the factors in each sphere to ensure they reflect current realities. As the external environment changes, some factors may shift in significance, necessitating adjustments to the mapping.

Conclusion

The spheres of influence framework provides a structured way to understand the various factors that affect an organization. By categorizing influences into Business, Micro, and Macro spheres, organizations can better assess risks, prioritize actions, and make informed decisions. Recognizing the diminishing level of control across these spheres is key to managing external risks while optimizing internal operations.

CHAPTER 10

Fusion

Fusion in the context of Cyber Threat Intelligence (CTI) is frequently misunderstood.[1] It is often perceived as the mere aggregation of disparate intelligence sources or the management of various random intelligence inputs. However, true fusion is a disciplined and strategic process that starts well before any data collection begins.[2] It is the deliberate act of identifying a specific threat or theme that you want to understand in greater depth and then methodically managing and deploying your collection assets to gather relevant intelligence.

Understanding Fusion: Beyond Data Aggregation

At its core, fusion is not just about managing a bundle of random intelligence. Instead, it is about establishing a clear, focused understanding of the threat landscape by defining specific intelligence needs and aligning

---

[1] SANS Institute, 2025 Cyber Threat Intelligence Survey—Key Findings (May 2025): Analysts cite "lack of process formalization" as the top barrier; many equate fusion with simple data aggregation. https://www.sans.org/white-papers/2025-cti-survey-webcast-forum-navigating-uncertainty-todays-threat-landscape/

[2] NIST, Special Publication 800-150—Guide to Cyber Threat Information Sharing (Oct 2016) §3.1: Recommends organizations "define sharing objectives and information needs before engaging in collection or exchange." https://csrc.nist.gov/pubs/sp/800/150/final

CHAPTER 10 FUSION

your collection assets accordingly. This process begins with a thorough introspective analysis: What is the exact threat you need to understand? What intelligence do you need to gather to mitigate that threat effectively?

This approach contrasts sharply with the practice of haphazardly collecting data from various sources without a clear purpose or strategy. True fusion is about precision—knowing exactly what you want to know and leveraging the right assets to obtain that knowledge.

The Process of Fusion: A Strategic Approach

1. **Identifying the Threat or Theme**: The fusion process starts with a clear understanding of the specific threat or theme you need to investigate. Whether it's phishing, ransomware, or nation-state actors, the first step is to clearly define the problem. This definition forms the foundation for all subsequent intelligence activities.

2. **Understanding Collection Assets**: Once the threat is identified, the next step is to understand the collection assets at your disposal. These assets could include anything from open-source intelligence (OSINT) tools, human intelligence (HUMINT), signals intelligence (SIGINT), or technical indicators from security systems. The key here is to understand which assets are best suited to collect the intelligence you need.

3. **Building Collection Assets Around the Threat**: Rather than starting with the tools or assets you already have, effective fusion means building or adapting your collection capabilities around the specific threat. For instance, if phishing is the threat, collection assets might include email filtering systems, honeypots designed to capture phishing emails, or monitoring of known phishing domains.

4. **Tasking and Managing Collection Assets**: Fusion involves more than just choosing the right tools; it's about effectively managing them. This means brokering the time with your assets—ensuring they are available and capable of performing the required tasks—and then tasking them with specific intelligence-gathering activities. Proper management ensures that the intelligence collected is relevant, timely, and actionable.

5. **Use Case Development and Requirements Definition**: Before acquiring or deploying collection assets, it is essential to spend time developing use cases and defining the requirements for each asset. This preemptive strategy ensures that when the asset is deployed, it is fully capable of answering the intelligence requirements tied to the identified threat.

Conclusion: The Essence of Fusion in CTI

Fusion in CTI is about precision, strategy, and purpose. It is a process that begins with a clear understanding of the threat and ends with the collection of targeted intelligence that directly addresses that threat.

CHAPTER 10 FUSION

This approach not only makes the intelligence process more efficient but also ensures that the insights gained are directly applicable to mitigating the identified risks.

By focusing on what you need to know and aligning your collection assets to meet these needs, fusion transforms from a misunderstood concept into a powerful tool for strategic intelligence gathering. It shifts the focus from merely managing information to actively directing intelligence efforts toward specific, actionable outcomes.

CHAPTER 11

PIRs (Prioritized Intelligence Requirements)

Introduction to Prioritized Intelligence Requirements (PIRs)

Prioritized Intelligence Requirements (PIRs) are a fundamental component of an effective Cyber Threat Intelligence (CTI) program. They serve as the foundation for all intelligence collection efforts and guide the focus of analysis and decision-making processes. Arriving at a list of PIRs that are both relevant and actionable is a critical step in the cybersecurity process, yet it is also one of the most challenging tasks for organizations of any size.

Understanding Intelligence Requirements

The first challenge in developing effective PIRs lies in understanding the intelligence requirements themselves. These requirements represent the specific information needs that, when met, will help an organization understand the threats it faces and make informed decisions. The intelligence requirements must be clearly defined and focused on the threat landscape relevant to the organization.

For example, an initial intelligence requirement might be as broad as, "What threat actors are targeting my organization?" This question serves as a starting point for deeper inquiries into specific threats and helps in shaping the overall intelligence strategy. The key to success at this stage is to avoid conflating intelligence requirements with internal control questions. PIRs should not be about evaluating internal security measures but rather about gathering external threat intelligence.

The Challenge of Prioritization

Once intelligence requirements are identified, the next step—prioritization—presents its own set of difficulties. Prioritization is essential because not all intelligence needs are of equal importance or urgency. The process involves evaluating which threats pose the greatest risk to the organization and focusing resources on addressing those first.

Prioritization is not a static process; it requires continuous assessment and adjustment as the threat landscape evolves. For instance, if an organization learns that a particular threat actor has escalated their activities against companies in the same sector, the PIRs might shift to focus more heavily on that specific actor's tactics, techniques, and procedures (TTPs).

PIRs Focused on Threats, Not Internal Controls

It's crucial to maintain the focus of PIRs on external threats. Questions should be directed at understanding and mitigating these threats rather than assessing internal controls. A well-crafted PIR might ask, "What are the main attack techniques used by threat actor X?" This type of question is designed to yield actionable intelligence that can inform defensive strategies.

Standing Tasks and Their Importance

Many PIRs are standing tasks, meaning they are ongoing and require regular updates. These standing PIRs ensure that critical intelligence needs are consistently addressed and that the organization remains vigilant to changes in the threat environment. For example, the question "What threat actors are targeting my organization?" might be a standing PIR that is revisited frequently to capture new developments.

Layering PIRs with Essential Elements of Intelligence (EEIs)

To make PIRs even more effective, they should be layered with sub-questions known as Essential Elements of Intelligence (EEIs). EEIs break down the main PIR into more specific, detailed questions that guide the collection and analysis process. For example, if the main PIR is, "What threat actors are targeting my organization?" an EEI might be, "What is the motivation behind these threat actors?" or "Which specific systems or data are they targeting?"

CHAPTER 11   PIRS (PRIORITIZED INTELLIGENCE REQUIREMENTS)

By using EEIs, organizations can ensure that their intelligence collection efforts are thorough and that the intelligence produced is both detailed and actionable.

Below are the top ten principles for creating PIRs:

1. Stay Focused on the Threat

PIRs should always address the external threat landscape, not internal tools or controls. The goal is to understand potential adversaries, their motivations, and capabilities. Ensuring that all PIRs are externally focused keeps the intelligence team aligned with understanding threats rather than operational performance.

2. A PIR is a Question, Not a Statement

PIRs should be framed as questions that seek to fill gaps in threat understanding. The question should aim to uncover who, what, where, when, and why, helping to understand adversaries, their objectives, and capabilities. For example, "What tactics, techniques, and procedures (TTPs) are likely to be used by the threat actors targeting our industry?"

3. Use Essential Elements of Information (EEIs)

Break down each PIR into sub-questions using Essential Elements of Information (EEIs) to support the primary intelligence requirement. EEIs add depth and structure to the PIR, making it easier to gather detailed intelligence. For instance, if a PIR is, "Who are the most likely threat actors to attack my organization?" an EEI might be, "What is the primary method of attack used by these threat actors?"

4. Prioritize PIRs and EEIs

Assign priority numbers to PIRs and EEIs to establish a clear hierarchy. This prioritization helps direct intelligence efforts toward the most pressing threats. Numbering the PIRs ensures that analysts can focus on gathering information with the greatest potential impact.

5. Classify PIRs as Sensitive Information

PIRs often reveal an organization's known weaknesses and intelligence gaps. Treat PIRs as sensitive information, applying the appropriate level of security classification to protect them from being disclosed to unauthorized individuals or groups.

6. Align PIRs with Key Threat Vectors

Build PIRs around the five main threat vectors: Phishing, Malware, Hacking, Distributed Denial of Service (DDoS), and Insider threats. Structuring PIRs this way ensures a comprehensive approach to understanding various threat types that could impact the organization.

7. Establish Metrics Around PIRs

Develop metrics to assess the effectiveness of the intelligence collected against each PIR. Metrics help measure the vendor's performance in answering the PIRs and provide an indication of how well the organization understands the threats.

8. Regularly Review and Update PIRs

Threats evolve, so it is essential to review PIRs regularly, such as on a monthly basis. Regular reviews ensure that PIRs remain relevant and aligned with the organization's current threat landscape and intelligence needs.

9. Incorporate Business Unit (BU) PIRs Without Bias

Understand the specific intelligence needs of different Business Units (BUs) and incorporate their PIRs into the overarching intelligence requirements. When integrating these, avoid favoritism to maintain an unbiased approach, ensuring that the organization's intelligence efforts remain balanced and comprehensive.

10. Label Intelligence Reports with the Relevant PIRs

Tag each intelligence report with the PIR it addresses. This practice helps maintain consistency, educate stakeholders, and ensure that the reports clearly align with organizational intelligence requirements, promoting a mature and structured approach to threat intelligence.

Conclusion: The Role of PIRs in Cyber Threat Intelligence

Effective PIRs guide intelligence collection and help organizations stay focused on understanding threats that pose the greatest risk. By following

CHAPTER 11   PIRS (PRIORITIZED INTELLIGENCE REQUIREMENTS)

these principles, organizations can build a robust intelligence framework that adapts to changing threats, supports informed decision-making, and enhances overall cybersecurity resilience.

PIRs are a critical tool in the CTI process, guiding the collection and analysis of threat intelligence. By carefully defining and prioritizing these requirements, organizations can ensure that their intelligence efforts are focused on the most pressing threats. The use of standing PIRs and the incorporation of EEIs further enhance the effectiveness of this process, ensuring that the intelligence gathered is relevant, timely, and actionable.

In summary, developing and managing PIRs is a complex but essential task that enables organizations to stay ahead of potential threats and make informed decisions to protect their assets.

CHAPTER 12

Intelligence Collection Plans (ICPs)

Intelligence Collection Plans (ICPs) are a critical component of the Cyber Threat Intelligence (CTI) framework, acting as the structured method by which Prioritized Intelligence Requirements (PIRs) are systematically addressed. An ICP aligns specific PIRs with the most appropriate intelligence collection assets, ensuring that the intelligence collected is both relevant and actionable. This process requires a deep understanding of each collection asset's capabilities to ensure they can effectively answer the PIRs and the associated Essential Elements of Intelligence (EEIs).

Populating the ICP: The Fusion of PIRs and Collection Assets

The creation of an ICP begins by populating it with the PIRs that have been identified as critical to the organization. Each PIR is then matched with the appropriate collection asset—whether it's a technological tool, a human intelligence source, or an open-source intelligence method—that is best suited to provide the required information. This alignment is the core function of the ICP, ensuring that each intelligence requirement is handled by the most capable resources available.

CHAPTER 12   INTELLIGENCE COLLECTION PLANS (ICPS)

Understanding Collection Asset Capabilities

A successful ICP hinges on a sound understanding of the capabilities and limitations of the collection assets at your disposal.[1] Not all assets are equally effective across all types of intelligence requirements, and it is crucial to align the right asset with the right PIR. For instance, a network monitoring tool may be highly effective at identifying malware communication patterns but may fall short when tasked with identifying the motivations behind a threat actor's actions. Therefore, the ICP must take into account the specific strengths and weaknesses of each asset.

Benefits of a Well-Executed ICP

When executed properly, an ICP not only facilitates the efficient collection of intelligence but also provides added benefits that can enhance an organization's overall security posture:

1. **Identifying Gaps and Inefficiencies**: If a collection asset consistently fails to provide the necessary intelligence to answer a PIR, this could indicate that the asset is not suitable for that particular task. This insight allows organizations to reassess the utility of their current tools and make informed decisions about future investments.

---

[1] US Air Force, AFDP 2-0—Intelligence (2023) Chap. 4: Emphasizes mapping available ISR assets to the commander's priorities, noting that "understanding the capabilities and limitations of each source is prerequisite to effective tasking." https://www.doctrine.af.mil/Doctrine-Publications/AFDP-2-0-Intelligence/

2. **Improving Vendor Selection and Cost Efficiency**:
   By identifying which collection assets are most effective, organizations can make better decisions when selecting vendors or acquiring new tools. This leads to more strategic investments, ensuring that resources are spent on assets that provide real value, thereby driving greater efficiency and cost savings over time.

3. **Enhancing Strategic Intelligence Gathering**:[2]
   A well-maintained ICP ensures that intelligence collection is not a reactive process but a proactive one. By continuously refining the ICP based on the results of previous intelligence efforts, organizations can better anticipate emerging threats and adjust their collection strategies accordingly.

Conclusion: The Strategic Importance of ICPs

Intelligence Collection Plans are the backbone of an effective CTI program, transforming abstract intelligence requirements into actionable data that can inform decision-making and threat mitigation efforts. By carefully matching PIRs with the most suitable collection assets, organizations can ensure that their intelligence operations are both efficient and effective. Moreover, the process of developing and refining an ICP offers valuable insights into the strengths and weaknesses of existing collection tools, guiding future investments and improving overall security outcomes.

---

[2] Joint Chiefs of Staff, Joint Publication 2-0—Joint Intelligence (22nd Oct 2013) Chap. 8: Defines collection management as "the discipline of knowing precisely what intelligence is required and tasking the right asset to collect it." https://www.jcs.mil/Doctrine/Joint-Doctrine-Pubs/2-0-Intelligence-Series/

CHAPTER 12   INTELLIGENCE COLLECTION PLANS (ICPS)

In summary, a well-executed ICP not only answers critical intelligence questions but also drives strategic improvements in an organization's CTI capabilities, leading to better protection against the ever-evolving landscape of cyber threats.

CHAPTER 13

Requests for Information (RFIs)

Outline the importance and process of RFIs in gathering necessary intelligence and filling information gaps.

Requests for Intelligence (RFIs) are one of the few intelligence practices that have transitioned from military to corporate environments[1] with minimal change in their fundamental purpose. An RFI is a formal request made to an intelligence team or source, aimed at answering a specific question that supports decision-making. However, in corporate settings, RFIs are frequently misunderstood or misused,[2] often mistaken as a request for information rather than for actionable intelligence.[3] For CTI

---

[1] Cloudflare's blog (8th Mar 2024) Cloudforce One outlined how RFIs and PIRs—originally military practices—now structure corporate threat intelligence operations as they did in defense contexts. https://blog.cloudflare.com/threat-intel-rfi-pir/

[2] SANS Institute Blog—"Beyond Meh-trics: Examining How CTI Programs Demonstrate Value Using Metrics" (9th Jan 2025): notes that many corporate teams "treat RFIs as generic information asks rather than actionable-intelligence tasks, leading to overload and low value." https://www.sans.org/blog/beyond-meh-trics-examining-how-cti-programs-demonstrate-value-using-metrics/

[3] According to Gartner's "Cyber Threat Intelligence: Use Cases and Success Factors" (22nd Nov 2023), organizations often confuse generic information inquiries with actionable intelligence requests, reducing RFI effectiveness. https://threatconnect.com/blog/empower-your-cti-a-3-step-guide-to-creating-intelligence-requirements-on-threatconnects-ti-ops-platform/

teams, properly managing RFIs is essential to ensuring that intelligence supports strategic priorities, improves threat response, and aligns with business goals.[4]

Ten fundamentals of RFI management in a CTI team include

1. **Assign an Analyst to Manage RFIs Daily.** Designate a dedicated analyst to handle RFIs each day. This role ensures requests are tracked, prioritized, and answered efficiently, helping maintain a structured approach to meeting the intelligence needs of the organization.

2. **Develop a Standardized RFI Template.** Create a standardized RFI template for all requests to streamline the process and avoid irrelevant or redundant fields. Customizing the template to CTI's needs prevents confusion and ensures requests align with the team's processes.

3. **Distinguish Between One-Off Requests and Standing Tasks.** Not all RFIs are one-time requests. Identify if an RFI is a single ad hoc inquiry or a recurring task that may fit within the broader intelligence collection plan. If it's an ongoing task, align it with the team's Prioritized Intelligence Requirements (PIRs) to avoid duplicating efforts.[5]

---

[4] Fortinet, MITRE Impact Report 2024 (15th Apr 2024): stresses that a governed RFI workflow "aligns intelligence output to strategic business priorities and measurable risk-reduction objectives." https://www.fortinet.com/blog/industry-trends/mitre-impact-report-2024-strengthening-threat-informed-defenses

[5] NATO AJP-2.1—Allied Joint Doctrine for Intelligence, Surveillance, and Reconnaissance (Ed. B, v1, 2015) Chap. 6: directs analysts to map recurring RFIs to standing PIRs to "avoid duplication and conserve limited analytic capacity."

4. **Set Clear and Reasonable Timelines.** Establish realistic expectations for response times based on the complexity of the RFI. Clear timelines allow both the CTI team and the requester to manage expectations and prioritize accordingly.

5. **Prioritize Based on Urgency and Business Impact.** Not all RFIs are equal, and urgency will vary. Explain where each RFI ranks within the broader cybersecurity priorities of the organization. This helps manage requesters' expectations, especially when multiple RFIs are competing for immediate attention.

6. **Make the RFI Service Accessible to the Entire Business.** Encourage transparency and inclusivity by making the RFI submission process accessible to all business units. Share links to the RFI template or portal so that all employees know how to submit requests for intelligence, fostering an open intelligence culture across the organization.

7. **Conduct Regular Customer Satisfaction Surveys.** Regularly gauge satisfaction with the RFI process through questionnaires or surveys. Feedback helps the CTI team improve processes, identify areas for enhancement, and ensure the RFI service meets the evolving needs of its users.

CHAPTER 13   REQUESTS FOR INFORMATION (RFIS)

8. **Commit to Continuous Improvement.** Managing RFIs effectively requires consistent effort. Actively seek ways to refine the process, manage workload efficiently, and improve the quality of responses. Treat each request as an opportunity to build trust and demonstrate the value of CTI to the organization.

9. **Engage with Stakeholders to Identify Key Concerns.** Regularly connect with stakeholders and leadership to understand their most pressing concerns. Knowing "what keeps them awake at night" helps CTI teams anticipate future RFIs, align with organizational priorities, and proactively address emerging risks.

10. **Use RFI Success Metrics to Evaluate Collection Assets.** Measure the success rate of RFI responses to assess the effectiveness of the CTI team's intelligence sources. These metrics help identify gaps in the collection process,[6] improve resource allocation, and ensure that the CTI team's assets are aligned with the intelligence needs of the organization.

---

[6] SANS Institute Blog—"Beyond Meh-trics: Examining How CTI Programs Demonstrate Value Using Metrics" (9th Jan 2025): "This becomes critical when conveying metrics over time, as people may erroneously fill in knowledge gaps that are unsupported by evidence." https://www.sans.org/blog/beyond-meh-trics-examining-how-cti-programs-demonstrate-value-using-metrics/

Conclusion

Proper RFI management is essential for an effective CTI program, allowing intelligence to be responsive, relevant, and actionable. By implementing these fundamentals, CTI teams can ensure that RFIs support the organization's intelligence needs while also building trust and demonstrating value across business units. Through structured processes, proactive engagement, and continuous improvement, RFIs can serve as a vital tool for informed decision-making and proactive threat management.

CHAPTER 14

Vendors

Selecting the right vendor for Cyber Threat Intelligence is a critical step in building a resilient cybersecurity posture.[1] Consider the role of third-party vendors in cybersecurity, including selecting and managing these relationships to enhance security posture.

Ten key principles to consider when selecting a CTI vendor:

1. What Is the Budget and Are There Any Hidden Costs?

Budget is the foundational consideration when selecting a vendor. Assess the total cost of ownership, including licensing, implementation, and training, and be mindful of potential hidden costs. These could include fees for accessing separate modules, RFIs, or usage-based charges. Ensure the vendor offers a transparent pricing structure to avoid surprises.[2]

---

[1] Forrester Wave: External Threat Intelligence Services, Q3 2023 (3rd Aug 2023). "External Threat Intelligence Is Necessary For Effective Cybersecurity": https://www.forrester.com/report/the-forrester-wave-tm-external-threat-intelligence-service-providers-q3-2023/RES178511

[2] Forrester Total Economic Impact™ (TEI) study—Trend Micro Security Platform (June 2021): shows TCO drivers such as modular add-ons and training fees. https://www.trendmicro.com/en_us/business/campaigns/total-economic-impact.html

2. Run a Clear and Well-Thought-Out RFP

A detailed, comprehensive RFP with specific requirements is essential. The vendor should demonstrate their capabilities in real-time scenarios, rather than relying on static PowerPoint presentations. This ensures that the solution aligns with your real-world needs and requirements.

3. Can They Answer Specific Prioritized Intelligence Requirements (PIRs)?

A CTI vendor should address your organization's specific intelligence requirements. Evaluate their ability to deliver relevant and timely intelligence aligned with your most pressing threats and risks, ensuring they can support your overall intelligence collection plan.

4. Reputation and Proven Expertise

Research the vendor's reputation and track record in the industry. Look for case studies, reviews, and examples from similar sectors to ensure that the vendor has proven expertise in delivering actionable intelligence.

5. Integration with Existing Security Tools and Scalability

Evaluate the vendor's ability to seamlessly integrate with your existing security tools, such as SIEM or endpoint detection systems. Additionally, ensure that the vendor's solution is scalable to grow with your organization's evolving needs and emerging threats without requiring significant overhauls.

6. Threat Coverage and Breadth of Intelligence

Assess the breadth and depth of the vendor's threat coverage. They should provide intelligence on a wide range of threat actors, vectors, and regions, covering the diverse nature of the threat landscape relevant to your business.

7. Data Accuracy and Relevance

The intelligence provided by the vendor must be accurate, timely, and relevant[3] to your organization's threat profile. Actionable, up-to-date intelligence is essential for responding to emerging threats in real time.

8. Customization and Flexibility

Ensure the vendor offers flexibility in their solution, allowing customization to fit your unique requirements. This ensures the solution can adapt to your specific operational context and security needs.

---

[3] Ponemon Institute, The Value of Threat Intelligence: Annual Study of North American and UK Companies (Feb 2019): 77% of respondents cite "difficulty integrating TI with existing security tools"; 59% flag concerns over data accuracy. https://www.anomali.com/es/resources/whitepapers/2019-ponemon-report-the-value-of-threat-intelligence-from-anomali

9. Support and Service Level Agreements (SLAs)

Look for strong customer support backed by clear SLAs.[4] Ensure that the vendor offers timely assistance and 24/7 support to help you operationalize intelligence and respond to incidents effectively.

10. Compliance with Industry Standards and Vendor Longevity

Ensure the vendor complies with relevant cybersecurity standards, such as NIST, ISO/IEC 27001,[5] or GDPR. Additionally, investigate their financial stability and roadmap to confirm they will be a long-term partner with a clear vision for future growth and development.

Conclusion

Vendor selection is not just about finding the right tool but ensuring it works seamlessly for your CTI analysts who will use the platform or Threat Intelligence Platform (TIP) daily. It is vital that your analysts have ample exposure to the tool before a final decision is made. Allow your team time to assess and evaluate the tool's simplicity, ease of use, and how quickly they can gather and utilize intelligence. Often, vendors assume their tool

---

[4] IDC Worldwide Security Services Survey Highlights (2022): 87% of organizations rank 24×7 vendor support and documented SLA metrics as "very important" when selecting threat-intel providers. https://my.idc.com/getdoc.jsp?containerId=US48851622

[5] ISO/IEC 27001 Information Security management Systems (ISMS) https://www.iso.org/standard/27001

is your top priority, overshadowing other intelligence sources in your Intelligence Collection Plan (ICP), if you have one.

Ensure the vendor can customize their services around your unique needs. For instance, you might not need the full platform but rather a dedicated analyst from the vendor's team, who already has access to the platform. This can be a cost-effective and viable alternative. Moreover, ensure that your team receives proper training on the service, directly from the vendor, as part of the contract. Comprehensive training is crucial for operationalizing the intelligence and maximizing the platform's value to your organization.

To continue further, when selecting a vendor, always remember

1. **Reassurance of Technical Superiority:** Your team needs to feel confident that they are working with the best, most advanced vendor in the field. This not only enhances their ability to work effectively but also reduces attrition. Analysts want to feel they are dealing with the highest level of intelligence, which keeps them engaged and prevents them from seeking new challenges elsewhere.

2. **Consideration of Intelligence Community Relationships:** If you have close relationships with other organizations or participate in intelligence-sharing communities, avoid relying on the same vendors that your peers use for similar threat coverage. Diversify your intelligence sources, but remember that vendors are bound by contract to provide accurate, timely intelligence. Sharing communities, while valuable, operate more on a basis of benevolence. You cannot justify to your board that a key piece of intelligence was missed because another organization failed to share it with you. This is called "*Competitive Collection.*"

CHAPTER 14 VENDORS

By adhering to these principles, you will not only select a CTI vendor that fits your current needs but also foster a partnership that supports your long-term security goals, while keeping your analysts engaged and your intelligence diverse and reliable.

CHAPTER 15

Intelligence Sources

Review various sources of intelligence, from open-source data to proprietary feeds, and how to leverage each type for maximum insight.

In Cyber, intelligence sources are the backbone of threat analysis and decision-making.[1] Unlike vendor selection, which involves specific use cases and formal RFP processes, managing intelligence sources requires a nuanced understanding of the diverse types of intelligence available and how to effectively integrate them into CTI workflows. This chapter covers the fundamentals of introducing and managing intelligence sources to create a cohesive, actionable intelligence program.

Ten Fundamentals of Managing Intelligence Sources

1. **Ensure the Intelligence is Guaranteed, Timely, and Accurate**: The core requirements for any intelligence source are accuracy, reliability, and timeliness. Intelligence that meets these criteria supports informed, confident decision-making. When selecting sources, prioritize those with a

---

[1] NIST Special Publication 800-150, Guide to Cyber Threat Information Sharing (Oct 2016)—§3.1 explains that "intelligence sources are foundational to timely, risk-based decision-making." https://csrc.nist.gov/pubs/sp/800/150/final

CHAPTER 15 INTELLIGENCE SOURCES

strong track record in accuracy and consistency,[2] ensuring the intelligence meets your organization's standards.

2. **Value Open Source Intelligence (OSINT) As a Primary Resource**: OSINT is a crucial intelligence source, often undervalued in organizations.[3] As a CTI team, it is essential to educate stakeholders on OSINT's value, from uncovering threat actor chatter to monitoring publicly available data. OSINT can be cost-effective, timely, and provide insights that proprietary sources may not, making it a valuable asset when used effectively. Remember the Deep Dark Web is OSINT, just as GitHub is too.

3. **Differentiate Between Paid Feeds and Shared Community Intelligence**: There is an important distinction between paid intelligence feeds from vendors and intelligence shared by communities, such as ISACs (Information Sharing and Analysis Centers). Community-shared intelligence is often firsthand and valuable, but it lacks contractual guarantees.[4] Paid intelligence feeds come with

---

[2] NCSC UK, *Evaluating Cyber Threat Intelligence Sources* (2023)—details accuracy, reliability, and timeliness criteria and recommends multisource corroboration. https://www.ncsc.gov.uk/collection/risk-management/threat-modelling

[3] SANS Institute, 2024 SANS CTI Survey (22nd May 2024)—76% of respondents cite OSINT as their most frequently used intelligence type; 63% rate it "high value." https://www.sans.org/webcasts/sans-2024-cti-survey-managing-the-evolving-threat-landscape/>

[4] FS-ISAC, Intelligence Sharing Practices for Financial Services (2022)—contrasts contractual SLAs of commercial feeds with community-based sharing via ISACs. https://www.fsisac.com/insights/tag/intelligence-sharing

service level agreements (SLAs) and are obligated to meet specific standards, providing a level of reliability that is essential in many CTI operations.

4. **Blend Intelligence Sources for Multisource Corroboration**: Relying on a single intelligence source is limiting and potentially risky. Use multiple sources to cross-verify information, building a multisource corroborated intelligence product. This approach enhances reliability and adds depth to intelligence analysis, ensuring a well-rounded view of the threat landscape.

5. **Consider the Method of Delivery and Accessibility**: Intelligence is only useful if it's accessible. Ensure that your team can access intelligence sources seamlessly, with minimal friction, through the chosen platform or tool. Whether through APIs, direct feeds, or vendor portals, streamline the process of accessing and consuming intelligence to ensure efficiency.

6. **Align Frequency and Delivery with Operational Needs**: Select intelligence sources that align with your operational tempo. Delays in intelligence delivery can result in outdated information, reducing its usefulness. Opt for sources that adhere to a "follow-the-sun" model if your team operates globally,[5] ensuring continuous coverage and relevance to ongoing activities.

---

[5] SANS Institute, 2022 SOC Survey (16th May 2022)—shows 68% of global SOCs require 24×7, follow-the-sun intelligence delivery to remain effective. https://www.sans.org/white-papers/sans-2022-soc-survey/

7. **Prioritize Intelligence Sources Based on PIRs and Relevance**: Intelligence prioritization is crucial to focus on what matters most to the organization. Set prioritization criteria based on PIRs, incident scale, and business relevance. If intelligence is actionable and relevant to your organization's security posture, it should be prioritized to enable swift responses and avoid potential incidents.

8. **Establish a Routine for Reading, Actioning, or Deleting Intelligence**: Intelligence should be regularly reviewed and acted upon to avoid missed opportunities or critical updates. Develop a structured workflow to ensure all incoming intelligence is consumed, assigned for action, or dismissed within a set time frame each day. Ignoring intelligence due to oversight or lack of routine is unacceptable, as it risks missing valuable insights.

9. **Avoid Bias in Selecting Intelligence Sources**: Bias in intelligence selection can lead to skewed or incomplete insights.[6] A balanced intelligence feed includes diverse sources without bias toward particular types of intelligence or regions. Bias-free selection supports a more objective understanding of the threat landscape, minimizing the risk of misinformation in finished intelligence products.

---

[6] RAND Corporation, Tradecraft Primer: Assessing the Value of Structured Analytic Techniques in the US Intelligence Community (9th Jan 2017) https://www.rand.org/pubs/research_reports/RR1408.html

10. **Select Intelligence Sources Over Information Feeds**: An intelligence source provides analysis, context, and actionable insights, whereas an information feed delivers raw data or news. Avoid selecting sources that merely push information, as this will overload analysts and dilute focus. Intelligence sources provide curated, analyzed content, saving analysts time and ensuring the feed remains actionable.

Applying These Fundamentals in Practice

To integrate these fundamentals into daily CTI practices, consider the following steps:

- **Map Intelligence Sources to PIRs**: Align intelligence sources with PIRs to ensure that they serve relevant CTI objectives. This helps prioritize sources and manage incoming intelligence effectively.

- **Regularly Review Source Effectiveness**: Intelligence needs evolve, and so should the sources. Assess each source periodically for accuracy, timeliness, and reliability to ensure that it continues to meet your team's requirements.

- **Promote Continuous Training**: Keep your team trained in using intelligence sources effectively, especially OSINT. Understanding the benefits and limitations of each source enables analysts to utilize them better.

CHAPTER 15 INTELLIGENCE SOURCES

Conclusion

The ability to source, blend, and manage intelligence effectively is a cornerstone of robust CTI operations. By following these fundamentals, CTI teams can create a well-rounded intelligence ecosystem that supports informed, accurate, and timely decision-making. As a result, organizations are better equipped to understand and respond to evolving cyber threats, enabling a proactive approach to security that aligns with business goals.

CHAPTER 16

Internal Control Data

Focus on how internal data, such as logs and error reports, can be mined for signs of security issues or breaches.

Internal control data is a valuable resource in any Cyber Threat Intelligence (CTI) program.[1] Although this data is not typically owned or managed by CTI teams, it plays a critical role when integrated with external intelligence sources. By correlating internal control data with external intelligence, CTI teams can enhance threat detection,[2] add context to incidents, and provide a more comprehensive understanding of the organization's threat landscape. Here are ten key fundamentals for CTI teams to consider when working with internal control data.

---

[1] NIST Special Publication 800-92, Guide to Computer Security Log Management (Sep 2006)—highlights internal logs as "critical sources of evidence for detecting security incidents."
https://csrc.nist.gov/pubs/sp/800/92/final

[2] SANS Institute, 2022 SOC Survey (16th May 2022)—72% of SOCs report that fusing internal telemetry with external intel improves detection accuracy, while 57% say it cuts false positives.
https://www.sans.org/white-papers/sans-2022-soc-survey/

CHAPTER 16   INTERNAL CONTROL DATA

Ten Fundamentals for Leveraging Internal Control Data in CTI

1. **Familiarize Yourself with the Internal Control Data Flow**: Before making any decisions or forming strategies, understand how internal control data flows within the organization. Identify the origins of data, how it's processed, and the channels it moves through. This knowledge provides a foundation for effectively integrating and utilizing the data.

2. **Do Not Become the Data Owner**: Gaining access to internal control data does not mean CTI must own it. Ownership typically involves management responsibilities that can become burdensome, especially with high volumes of unprocessed data. Instead, agree with the control owner on access and usage, clarifying that CTI's role is to analyze and correlate rather than maintain the data.

3. **Collaborate with Control Owners During Procurement**: Engage with control owners during the requirements phase of procurement. By including CTI's requirements and use cases in the initial list, CTI teams can avoid future issues around data accessibility and shadow IT. This proactive approach also ensures that new tools align with the organization's intelligence and security needs from the start.

4. **Align Internal Control Data with the Big 5 Threat Vectors**: Link internal control data sources to the primary threat vectors:

    - **Phishing**: Utilize email security software.

    - **Malware**: Leverage Endpoint Detection and Response (EDR) tools.

    - **Hacking and Vulnerabilities**: Draw insights from vulnerability management systems.[3]

    - **DDoS**: Collaborate with network security teams and Internet Service Providers (ISPs).

    - **Insider Threats**: Integrate Data Loss Prevention (DLP) tools.

    This alignment ensures that data is relevant to the key threats CTI monitors.

5. **Add Context to Internal Control Data**: CTI's role is to provide context to data. Determining whether an email or malware attack is unique to the organization or part of a broader threat pattern is crucial. This context helps assess the severity of incidents and informs the appropriate level of response.

---

[3] Verizon, 2024 Data Breach Investigations Report—maps the majority of confirmed breaches to the same five primary vectors (phishing, malware, hacking, DDoS, insider) you reference. https://www.verizon.com/business/resources/reports/dbir/

CHAPTER 16   INTERNAL CONTROL DATA

6. **Automate the Intelligence Feed from Internal Controls**: Streamlining data collection by automating feeds from internal controls ensures timely and consistent access[4] to relevant information. Automation reduces manual intervention, allowing CTI analysts to focus on analyzing rather than managing data.

7. **Ensure Access to Historical and Real-Time Data**: Access to both current and historical data enables trend analysis and predictive modeling.[5] Having a comprehensive data timeline helps CTI teams identify patterns, track threat evolution, and improve incident response accuracy.

8. **Minimize False Positives**: Work closely with control owners to filter out false positives.[6] Collaborate to refine the data, ensuring that CTI receives actionable information. Effective filtering prevents unnecessary workloads for analysts and allows them to focus on genuine threats.

---

[4] IBM, Cost of a Data Breach Report 2024—finds organizations that deploy automated, real-time security analytics shorten breach lifecycle by 108 days on average. https://www.ibm.com/reports/data-breach

[5] Mandiant, M-Trends 2024—stresses the value of multi-year endpoint and log data for spotting attacker dwell-time patterns (median dwell time reported at 10 days, down from 16). https://cloud.google.com/blog/topics/threat-intelligence/m-trends-2024

[6] SANS Institute, 2022 SOC Survey (16th May 2022)—72% of SOCs report that fusing internal telemetry with external intel improves detection accuracy, while 57% say it cuts false positives.
https://www.sans.org/white-papers/sans-2022-soc-survey/

9. **Educate Architects and Engineers on Data Accessibility**: Data availability is key to effective intelligence gathering. Engage with engineers to understand if security systems are set to detect and delete threats, as this could result in data loss. Emphasize the importance of retaining information about attempted breaches, as it can provide valuable insights for trend analysis and future planning.

10. **Promote the Value of Integrated Intelligence to Stakeholders**: Share integrated intelligence insights with stakeholders, particularly leadership. By showcasing the comprehensive view that internal and external data correlation provides, CTI teams can build demand and appreciation for these insights, making it essential for decision-making.

Conclusion

Integrating internal control data into CTI provides a layered view of the organization's threat landscape. By understanding data flow, collaborating with control owners, automating feeds, and adding context, CTI teams can enhance threat detection and analysis. When internal control data is effectively integrated with external intelligence, the organization gains a holistic view of its security posture, enabling proactive threat management and more informed strategic decisions.

CHAPTER 17

Intelligence Sharing

Promote the benefits and methodologies of sharing intelligence across organizations and with external entities to bolster collective security efforts.

Intelligence sharing, by nature, can seem paradoxical.[1] Intelligence is traditionally seen as sensitive information, valuable precisely because it is carefully guarded. The notion of sharing intelligence often raises concerns about reducing its value or inadvertently increasing the vulnerability of the data owner. However, in military contexts, intelligence sharing has long been essential, driven by the belief that collaborative insight strengthens collective defense and that certain intelligence may be valuable to others. An example of this collaboration is the "Five Eyes" (FVEY) alliance,[2] comprising Australia, Canada, New Zealand, the USA, and the UK, which operates under formal agreements to share intelligence across allied nations.

---

[1] US Office of the Director of National Intelligence (ODNI), Strategic Intent for Information Sharing (2011–2015)—explains the "inherent tension" between safeguarding and sharing intelligence.
https://www.dni.gov/files/documents/Newsroom/Reports%20and%20Pubs/IC_Information_Sharing_Strategy.pdf

[2] Forbes "What Is The Five Eyes Alliance?" https://www.forbes.com/advisor/business/what-is-five-eyes/

CHAPTER 17   INTELLIGENCE SHARING

In the corporate world, formal intelligence-sharing agreements do not exist to the same extent. Instead, businesses share intelligence through mechanisms like the Information Sharing and Analysis Centers (ISACs)[3] or sector-specific trusted communities, either on a paid or voluntary basis. Paid platforms offer advantages like anonymity, access control, and secure sharing, though true anonymity cannot always be guaranteed when certain parties have visibility into who is sharing what information. While intelligence sharing in the corporate world remains relatively immature compared to governmental practices, its importance is growing. Below are ten key fundamentals for intelligence sharing that a CTI team should consider.

Ten Fundamentals of Intelligence Sharing in CTI

1. **Classify and Mark the Intelligence**: Before sharing intelligence, classify it appropriately and mark it with the correct sensitivity level. This practice helps ensure the data is handled according to security protocols and reduces the risk of unintentional exposure. **Use a Standardized Security Classification System.** Ensure that all parties involved in intelligence sharing understand

---

[3] CISA, Information Sharing and Analysis Centers (ISACs)—program description and sector list.
https://www.cisa.gov/topics/cyber-threats-and-advisories/information-sharing/information-sharing-vital-resource

the security classifications used. The Traffic Light Protocol (TLP)[4] is a widely accepted standard:

- **Green**: Intelligence can be shared within the broader organization.
- **Amber**: Share only within a trusted circle.
- **Red**: For your eyes only, unless there is an imminent, direct danger to the business.

2. **Connect with the Receiver Before Sharing**: Always communicate with the intended recipient beforehand to clarify expectations and minimize the risk of mishandling. By doing so, the receiver can prepare to handle the intelligence with the appropriate caution.

3. **Classify and Grade the Quality of the Intelligence**: Always communicate with the intended recipient the quality, accuracy, and reliability of the source. The Admiralty Code is a widely recognized system.[5]

4. **Only Join Intelligence-Sharing Communities if You Intend to Participate**: Membership in intelligence-sharing communities requires active contributions. Organizations that participate without contributing weaken the collaborative value and may not fully benefit from the insights shared by others.

---

[4] FIRST.org, Traffic Light Protocol (TLP) Version 2.0 specification. https://www.first.org/tlp/

[5] UK MOD, Joint Doctrine Publication 2-00: Understanding and Intelligence Support to Joint Operations (17th Aug 2013) p. 59—NATO Intelligence Grading System
https://www.gov.uk/government/publications/jdp-2-00-understanding-and-intelligence-support-to-joint-operations

5. **Adopt a "Need to Know" Policy**: Even with classifications in place, always assess the necessity of sharing intelligence within your organization. Just because intelligence is marked as "Green" does not mean it should be widely disseminated. This approach minimizes the risk of unauthorized or unnecessary access.

6. **Recognize Regulatory Expectations**: Regulatory bodies expect organizations of certain sizes and security capabilities to engage in intelligence sharing[6] and to demonstrate these practices. Showing regulators that your organization participates in intelligence-sharing networks can help meet compliance requirements.

7. **Intelligence Sharing Strengthens Business Resilience**: As businesses aim to build resilience against cyber threats, intelligence sharing will continue to grow in importance.[7] Access to shared intelligence enhances situational awareness, supporting proactive threat detection and response.

8. **Consider Visibility Among Competitors**: Being seen as open and transparent within the industry can benefit the business, particularly among competitors. Intelligence sharing can foster

---

[6] EU Directive (EU) 2022/2555 (NIS 2) Article 29—mandates cyber-threat "information sharing and cooperation" among essential entities. https://eur-lex.europa.eu/eli/dir/2022/2555/oj

[7] World Economic Forum, Global Cybersecurity Outlook 2023—91% of executives say intelligence sharing "improves overall cyber-resilience." https://www.weforum.org/reports/global-cybersecurity-outlook-2023/

trust and enhance the organization's reputation as a collaborative and security-conscious industry player.

9. **Share Only Finished CTI Intelligence**: Avoid sharing raw intelligence data without added analysis or context. Unfiltered intelligence may be misinterpreted or taken out of context. When necessary, provide commentary that ties the intelligence to business-specific insights to ensure clarity and relevance.

10. **Limit CTI Vendor Intelligence Access to CTI Teams**: Vendor intelligence should be handled exclusively by the CTI team. Allowing access to external teams or non-CTI individuals can create redundant reporting, misinterpretations, and divergent conclusions. The CTI team should be solely responsible for analyzing vendor feeds and disseminating intelligence within the organization.

Conclusion

Intelligence sharing is an essential component of modern cyber threat intelligence, strengthening security through collaboration and mutual insight. By following these fundamentals, CTI teams can ensure that intelligence is shared responsibly, securely, and strategically, fostering resilience and reinforcing a culture of informed collaboration within the industry.

CHAPTER 18

The Cyber Criminal

The cyber threat landscape has evolved significantly over recent years, becoming more complex and harder to navigate. Today, organizations contend with a broad array of threats: from lone opportunistic hackers to highly organized cybercrime gangs, ideological hacktivists, and covert state-sponsored actors known as Advanced Persistent Threats (APTs). What was once niche and specialist is now widely accessible—tools and access can be purchased, rented, or stolen with relative ease.[1] Threats have become increasingly commoditized and monetized,[2] with malware, phishing kits, and access brokers flooding dark web marketplaces.

This new era of cybercrime introduces an industrialized and scalable adversary model. And with attackers hiding behind obfuscation, proxies, and shared tooling, attribution[3] becomes both difficult and often irrelevant. In this environment, Cyber Threat Intelligence (CTI) teams

---

[1] Palo Alto Networks Unit 42, 2023 Threat Report—credential reuse is common on IT and security infrastructure, which means that attacks can be heavily automated and don't require an unpatched vulnerability to succeed. https://www.paloaltonetworks.com/resources/research/2023-unit-42-attack-surface-threat-report

[2] Recorded Future, 2024 Malicious Infrastructure Report (25th Feb 2025)—malware-as-a-service (MaaS) infostealers, led by LummaC2, grew in prevalence, likely driven by law enforcement actions against competitor infostealers and rapid innovation by LummaC2. https://www.recordedfuture.com/research/2024-malicious-infrastructure-report

[3] RAND Corporation, Promoting Accountability in Cyberspace https://www.rand.org/nsrd/projects/cyberspace-accountability.html

CHAPTER 18   THE CYBER CRIMINAL

must focus on the behavioral signatures of adversaries—their techniques, tactics, and procedures (TTPs)—rather than chasing attribution.

To effectively navigate this shifting landscape, CTI teams must adapt. The following ten key considerations outline a modern approach to understanding cybercriminal activity, supported by clarity around APTs, supply chain threats, insider risk, ransomware proliferation, and evolving attack surfaces.

Ten Key Considerations for Navigating the Cyber Environment

1. **Attribution Is Difficult—And Often Irrelevant**: Attributing attacks to specific actors is complicated by shared infrastructure, code reuse, and intentional misdirection (false flags). Rather than obsessing over naming the group behind an attack, CTI teams should focus on understanding TTPs. Frameworks like MITRE ATT&CK[4] help analysts assess behaviors and build detection strategies that are applicable regardless of actor identity.

2. **Malware Is a Commodity**: Malware is no longer bespoke to the actor that first developed it.[5] Variants and payloads are traded, leaked, or repurposed. What matters is understanding the role of the

---

[4] MITRE ATT&CK® knowledge base—official site detailing tactics, techniques, and procedures.
https://attack.mitre.org/

[5] Sophos, Sophos Threat Report 2024—notes that commodity malware families (Emotet, Qakbot) appeared in 36% of incidents, regardless of originating actor.
https://news.sophos.com/en-us/2024/03/12/2024-sophos-threat-report/

malware in the attack chain—is it initial access, a dropper, lateral movement, or a second-stage payload? Malware should be profiled based on its utility and stage in the intrusion set, not its branding.

3. **Cybercrime Gangs Operate like a Workforce**: Modern cybercrime groups function as organized commercial entities. They feature hierarchies, recruitment practices, customer support teams, and brand awareness campaigns. Adversaries move between these groups just like employees in a workforce, taking with them preferred TTPs and toolsets. This horizontal movement spreads methodologies across criminal ecosystems, complicating actor profiling.

4. **Not All APTs Are Alike**: Advanced Persistent Threats (APTs) are typically state-sponsored or state-tolerated groups operating with long-term objectives, such as espionage, sabotage, or influence operations. Unlike cybercriminals motivated by profit, APTs pursue strategic outcomes and often display persistence, patience, and high operational security. However, APTs differ in capability, scope, and structure. Some are tightly integrated into military units, while others are contractor-based cells operating semi-independently. This distinction matters when assessing risk to critical infrastructure or national interests.

CHAPTER 18   THE CYBER CRIMINAL

5. **Increased Attack Frequency, Lower Impact on Prepared Organizations**: The volume of attacks will continue to rise, but the impact on mature, well-prepared organizations may diminish—provided defenses and CTI reporting are well-structured. CTI teams should not become overwhelmed by noise. Instead, they must learn to filter low-priority events and focus on those with true potential for business disruption.

6. **State-Sponsored Targeting of Supply Chains**: Nation-state actors frequently target supply chains and Critical National Infrastructure (CNI) to achieve strategic objectives indirectly. These attacks are subtle, systemic, and deeply embedded. CTI teams should monitor not only their own organization, but also trusted third parties and downstream dependencies. This includes technology vendors, cloud services, and contractors.

7. **Insider Threats and External Recruitment**: Insiders represent an ongoing and underappreciated threat. Whether acting maliciously, negligently, or under coercion, insiders can be exploited by cybercriminal groups. There is growing evidence of OCGs recruiting insiders via social engineering or financial incentive. CTI must liaise with Identity and Access Management (IAM) and Data Loss Prevention (DLP) teams to detect early signs of abnormal behavior.

8. **Third-Party Breaches and Cascading Risks**: Threats can cascade across trust boundaries. Even when your own network is secure, third-, fourth-, and fifth-party vendors may expose your data or systems. It's essential to understand the supply chain map and monitor your most sensitive and interconnected partners. Visibility reduces with each degree of separation.

9. **Rapid Exploitation of Vulnerabilities**: The time between public disclosure and exploitation is shrinking.[6] Proof-of-concept (PoC) code is weaponized almost immediately upon publication. CTI must establish clear and fast communication with patching and vulnerability management teams to mitigate risk during this crucial window.

10. **Dormant, Low-Profile Threats Are Increasingly Common**: Sophisticated adversaries don't always announce their presence. Some breaches are designed to be invisible, maintaining long-term access while gathering intelligence, siphoning data, or mapping systems. These threats are often only uncovered through proactive threat hunting and telemetry analysis. CTI must account for both loud and silent compromises.

---

[6] Rapid7, Vulnerability Intelligence Report 2023—56% of exploits occurred within seven days of CVE publication; some within 24 hours. https://investors.rapid7.com/news/news-details/2023/Rapid7-Vulnerability-Intelligence-Report-Shows-Attackers-Developing-and-Deploying-Exploits-Faster-Than-Ever/

CHAPTER 18   THE CYBER CRIMINAL

Ransomware: The Criminal Weapon of Choice

Ransomware has become the hallmark of modern cybercrime. It combines operational ease, scalable monetization, and devastating impact. Ransomware-as-a-Service (RaaS) platforms allow criminal affiliates to launch attacks with minimal technical expertise.[7] These platforms offer built-in payloads, encryption tools, and dark web support channels, allowing attackers to focus on access and extortion.

Ransomware gangs now operate like extortion businesses—with dedicated negotiation teams, public leak sites, and pressuring tactics, including threats of regulatory disclosure. Industries most frequently targeted include healthcare, education, local government, and critical infrastructure[8]—sectors often underfunded in cybersecurity but rich in data and urgency.

What sets ransomware apart is its ability to scale criminal profits while also disrupting entire ecosystems. From locking hospitals and halting city operations to extorting multinational corporations, ransomware continues to evolve as a primary tool for financially motivated threat actors.

CTI teams must

- Track affiliate campaigns and ransomware variants.

- Profile initial access vectors and lateral movement techniques.

---

[7] Palo Alto Networks Unit 42, Ransomware & Extortion Report 1H 2024—lists 60+ active RaaS programs and a 49% YoY rise in affiliate-driven attacks. https://unit42.paloaltonetworks.com/unit-42-ransomware-leak-site-data-analysis/

[8] IBM Security, X-Force Threat Intelligence Index 2025—Healthcare, Education, Government, and Energy topped the list of ransomware-targeted sectors. https://www.ibm.com/reports/threat-intelligence

- Prioritize PIRs that assess ransomware activity against sector-specific threats.

- Coordinate with IR and SOC teams to ensure visibility on ransomware behaviors.

- Report not just on the payloads but also on the adversarial infrastructure and negotiation playbooks being used.

Conclusion: A Criminal Ecosystem, Not Just a Battlefield

The modern cyber environment is less of a warzone and more of an ecosystem—where criminal gangs operate like businesses, APTs wage strategic campaigns in the shadows, and tools are recycled, reused, and resold at scale. The borders between actor types are increasingly porous, with cybercrime enabling statecraft and vice versa.

The CTI analyst's role is not to solve attribution riddles, but to map the threat landscape in motion, assess what matters most to the business, and report on how adversary behaviors evolve.

Understanding how malware spreads, why attackers choose specific targets, and how third parties may expose an organization is more valuable than a list of group names. By focusing on TTPs, adversary motivations, ransomware proliferation, supply chain dependencies, and insider risk, CTI teams can help organizations adapt and respond faster than their adversaries can evolve.

CHAPTER 19

Scenarios for Testing

Introducing scenario-based testing as a method for assessing the effectiveness of cybersecurity measures and preparing for potential breaches.

Cyber threat scenarios are an increasingly essential function within CTI teams,[1] providing a valuable service to the broader cybersecurity team. Scenarios allow teams to simulate real-world attack patterns, test defenses, and improve incident response strategies. However, scenarios are often created in isolation by siloed teams or departments focused on testing specific tools or meeting compliance requirements. When designed without a comprehensive threat intelligence perspective, these scenarios may inadvertently create unrealistic threat models or biased tests focused on a specific tool's capabilities.

For a scenario to be truly valuable, it should reflect the current threat landscape, be grounded in real-world TTPs, and offer a complete, end-to-end view of an attack.[2] CTI teams are ideally positioned to design

---

[1] NIST Special Publication 800-115, Technical Guide to Information Security Testing and Assessment (23rd Apr 2021)—§2.2 recommends scenario-based exercises to "evaluate the effectiveness of security controls and incident response capabilities." https://www.nist.gov/privacy-framework/nist-sp-800-115

[2] SANS Institute, Cyber Threat Intelligence Survey 2024—over 95% of respondents utilizing MITRE ATT&CK framework for categorizing and communicating tactics, techniques, and procedures (TTPs).
https://www.sans.org/press/announcements/unveiling-key-findings-sans-institute-2024-cyber-threat-intelligence-survey/

these scenarios accurately and ensure they are relevant and based on intelligence rather than hypothetical tool-centric risks. Here are ten best practices for writing effective cyber threat scenarios.

Ten Best Practices for Writing Cyber Threat Scenarios

1. **Design Scenarios with an End-to-End Perspective**: A cyber threat scenario should encompass the full attack life cycle, from initial access to lateral movement, persistence, and data exfiltration. End-to-end scenarios help ensure a realistic test of defenses across multiple stages, capturing a holistic view of the organization's security posture.

2. **Select Relevant and Hypothetical Attack Models**: Scenarios do not need to replicate attacks that have already occurred within the organization. Instead, choose hypothetical attacks based on relevant industry threats or observed tactics used by known adversaries. This approach allows the CTI team to prepare for plausible attack scenarios even if the organization has not yet encountered them directly.

3. **Test Against New Defensive Layers or Mitigations**: If your scenario is created in response to a recent change in the defensive layer or to test an enhanced mitigation tool post-breach, ensure it aligns with the new capabilities. For example, if new endpoint detection mechanisms are in place, include techniques within the scenario that challenge these defenses to validate their effectiveness.

4. **Align with the MITRE ATT&CK Framework**: Using the MITRE ATT&CK framework helps map attack techniques to real-world TTPs, providing a structured, intelligence-driven approach to scenario design. This alignment allows the CTI team to simulate relevant techniques and evaluate the organization's defenses at various attack stages.

5. **Avoid Tool-Centric Scenarios**: Scenarios should be written without an emphasis on any single tool or defensive technology. When scenarios are biased toward testing a specific tool, they may lead to a narrow assessment, which doesn't accurately reflect the organization's broader threat landscape. Focus instead on simulating a realistic attack path that tests multiple layers of defense.

6. **Incorporate Diverse Attack Vectors**: Include multiple attack vectors within scenarios to challenge the organization's defenses from various angles.[3] For example, a phishing attack followed by credential harvesting, lateral movement, and privilege escalation offers a richer assessment of the organization's defenses compared to a single-vector scenario.

7. **Define Clear Objectives and Success Criteria**: Each scenario should have clear objectives, such as evaluating detection capabilities, incident response, or assessing resilience to lateral movement.

---

[3] IBM Security, X-Force Threat Intelligence Index 2024—notes 85% of breaches involved "multiple attack vectors within a single intrusion chain." https://www.ibm.com/reports/threat-intelligence

CHAPTER 19   SCENARIOS FOR TESTING

> Define success criteria up-front so that the results of the scenario can be effectively measured and analyzed, leading to actionable improvements.

8. **Integrate Intelligence from Real-World Incidents**: Base scenarios on real-world incidents when possible.[4] Observing actual cyber events in the industry can provide valuable insights into the attack methods most likely to impact your organization. Use data from recent incidents to inform the tactics, techniques, and procedures (TTPs) included in the scenario.

9. **Simulate the Threat Beyond Initial Access**: Avoid limiting scenarios to initial access alone. While the ability to detect and block an initial attempt is important, focusing on what would happen if the initial attempt succeeds provides deeper insights. Testing lateral movement, privilege escalation, and data exfiltration capabilities ensures defenses are prepared[5] for a range of possible outcomes.

10. **Share Findings with Stakeholders to Drive Improvements**: Once a scenario is completed, share the results with relevant stakeholders, including lessons learned and areas for improvement. Clearly communicate how the

---

[4] Verizon, 2024 Data Breach Investigations Report—provides incident data and TTPs that can be directly converted into realistic test scenarios. https://www.verizon.com/business/resources/reports/dbir/

[5] Mandiant, M-Trends 2024—emphasizes that defenders must evaluate response to post-exploitation stages such as lateral movement and exfiltration; median dwell time now 10 days, underscoring need for deep scenarios. https://cloud.google.com/blog/topics/threat-intelligence/m-trends-2024

findings apply to the organization's broader security goals. Use this opportunity to reinforce the importance of a realistic, threat-based approach to cybersecurity within the organization.

Conclusion

Creating realistic, comprehensive cyber threat scenarios is a vital function for CTI teams, allowing organizations to test defenses and prepare for potential cyber events. By following these best practices, CTI teams can design scenarios that provide valuable insights into the organization's preparedness, resilience, and response capabilities. Scenarios grounded in threat intelligence, based on real-world techniques, and free from tool-centric biases are essential for strengthening the organization's cybersecurity posture.

CHAPTER 20

End to End Process

Examine the end-to-end process of identifying, analyzing, and mitigating cyber threats within an organization.

An "end-to-end" process in cybersecurity refers to the comprehensive strategy set out by the CISO or Head of Cybersecurity,[1] ensuring that all cybersecurity elements work cohesively to protect the organization. CTI is one critical component within this broader strategy, not an end-to-end process itself, but part of an integrated sequence that moves from understanding external threats to detecting, responding, and recovering from incidents.

This end-to-end strategy begins with direction from the CISO, guiding all cybersecurity teams to align with the organization's security objectives. CTI plays an essential role in initiating this "relay" by providing intelligence insights, but it is equally important that the intelligence team knows when to "pass the baton" to the next team. A coordinated handoff helps to ensure that each team is aware of where the process stands,[2] so if

---

[1] NIST Cybersecurity Framework v1.1 (April 2018)—Core Function "Identify" notes that an organization-wide, end-to-end strategy must be led by executive cybersecurity leadership.
https://www.nist.gov/cyberframework/csf-11-archive

[2] NIST Special Publication 800-61 r3, Incident Response Recommendations and Considerations for Cybersecurity Risk Management: A CSF 2.0 Community Profile (Apr 2025)—§3.2 emphasizes clear phase handoffs and re-engagement of threat-intel staff via RFIs during response.
https://csrc.nist.gov/pubs/sp/800/61/r3/final

CHAPTER 20   END TO END PROCESS

any step encounters a delay, all teams can adjust accordingly. Throughout the process, CTI may be re-engaged via RFIs (Requests for Intelligence) to provide updated intelligence, keeping the strategy dynamic and responsive.

Below are ten fundamentals that a CTI team should follow to effectively support an end-to-end cybersecurity strategy.

Ten Fundamentals for CTI Within an End-to-End Cybersecurity Strategy

1. **Seek a Clear Strategy from Senior Leadership**: The CTI team should operate within the end-to-end framework set by senior leadership, ideally the CISO. A clear, top-down strategy defines the CTI team's priorities, focus areas, and critical threats, ensuring CTI insights directly support the organization's broader security objectives.

2. **Understand CTI's Role within the End-to-End Strategy**: CTI's role is to provide actionable intelligence insights that initiate the end-to-end process, preparing downstream teams to act. By understanding how CTI contributes to this strategy, the team can ensure intelligence serves as a foundation for coordinated defense without overstepping its role.

3. **Use the Intelligence Life Cycle to Build CTI SOPs**: Structure CTI's standard operating procedures (SOPs) around the intelligence life cycle.[3]

    - **Direction**: Define CTI's focus based on the CISO's guidance.

    - **Collection**: Gather relevant data and intelligence to inform the organization's security posture.

    - **Analysis**: Produce actionable intelligence that provides context to identified threats.

    - **Dissemination**: Hand off intelligence to the appropriate teams in the workflow, allowing them to act on the insights CTI provides.

4. **Collaborate Consistently with Operational Teams**: Regular communication with SOC, incident response, and control teams promotes visibility and prevents gaps in the process. If CTI is the first "leg" of the relay, downstream teams should be aware of when and how intelligence insights are handed off, allowing for seamless transitions and minimizing response delays.

5. **Focus on Operational Delivery, Not Project Work**: Operational focus ensures that CTI efforts directly contribute to the security posture. Avoid becoming distracted by projects that develop new

---

[3] MITRE Engenuity, Understanding the Cyber-Threat Intelligence Cycle (2021)—describes Direction, Collection, Processing/Analysis, and Dissemination as the foundation for CTI SOPs.
https://www.dragos.com/resources/reports/exec-guide-mitre-engenuity-attack-evaluations/

CHAPTER 20   END TO END PROCESS

tools or systems, as these are outside the end-to-end workflow. While projects build capacity, operational work ensures intelligence insights actively support the end-to-end process.

6. **Know When to Pass the Baton**: Like a relay, CTI needs to know when to stop and pass the baton to the next team in the workflow. The CTI team initiates the intelligence phase, but operational actions are passed on to other cybersecurity teams. All team members should be able to see where the baton is on its journey to completion. If delays arise, teams can quickly identify where they occur and adjust. CTI should be prepared to re-engage at any point if additional intelligence is needed, possibly through an RFI.

7. **Select Vendors Aligned with the Entire End-to-End Process**: Invest in vendors that contribute to the full end-to-end process. Vendors that integrate with platforms like SOAR and SIEM can help automate information-sharing,[4] ensuring intelligence insights flow smoothly between CTI and downstream teams.

8. **Recognize CTI as a Support Function, Not an Authority**: CTI supports the broader mission rather than leading the process. Effective CTI provides value by adding context to decision-making without competing for authority. Avoid positioning CTI as

---

[4] CISA, New Guidance for SIEM and SOAR Implementation (27th May 2025) https://www.cisa.gov/news-events/alerts/2025/05/27/new-guidance-siem-and-soar-implementation

a sole authority; instead, focus on enhancing the organization's overall security posture.

9. **Plan Resource Allocation for Global Coverage**: For globally dispersed teams, "follow-the-sun" models ensure round-the-clock intelligence monitoring and response.[5] This approach provides the necessary coverage to meet the end-to-end strategy's needs, allowing CTI to respond in real time to emerging threats across different regions.

10. **Test Processes Regularly to Ensure Cohesion**: Regular testing of processes across CTI and operational teams allows for seamless integration, ensuring each team fulfills its role within the end-to-end strategy. Testing identifies and addresses process gaps, strengthens collaboration, and prepares teams to respond cohesively in a real-world scenario.

Intelligence As the Catalyst in End-to-End Strategy

In the end-to-end strategy, CTI operates as a starting point and catalyst, offering critical insights that set other teams into action. Intelligence-led decision-making empowers teams with situational awareness, guiding the entire security response. However, CTI's role is to provide insights, not lead the operation. This relationship is similar to military intelligence, where intelligence informs strategy, but operational execution remains with operations.

---

[5] SANS 2022 SOC Survey—68% of global SOCs employ a follow-the-sun model to maintain 24×7 monitoring and intel support.
https://www.sans.org/white-papers/sans-2022-soc-survey/

CHAPTER 20   END TO END PROCESS

Deception As a Defensive Tactic

CTI's role remains defensive, and deception tactics—such as honeypots—can be used to divert adversaries. A carefully designed honeypot environment can create a realistic environment for the attacker,[6] leading them to believe they have breached critical systems. This approach allows forensic teams to monitor and study the attack in a controlled setting, minimizing risk to production environments.

Conclusion

An end-to-end cybersecurity strategy aligns all teams to a common goal, fostering cohesion and improving resilience against cyber threats. By understanding and following these fundamentals, CTI teams can ensure that intelligence serves as an effective starting point within the cybersecurity framework, setting downstream teams up for success. Clear handoffs, continuous communication, and a focus on the intelligence life cycle allow CTI to function as a critical support element, aligning seamlessly with the CISO's overarching vision.

---

[6] MITRE Engage Matrix—"Deception & Adversary Engagement" tactics include deploying honeypots to divert and study attackers in a controlled environment. https://engage.mitre.org/matrix/

CHAPTER 21

Heat Maps

Heat maps are used to visually represent areas of higher threat density or vulnerability within an organization.

Heat maps are an effective tool for visually representing the threat landscape,[1] offering CTI teams a clear, concise way to communicate the position and trajectory of threats to stakeholders, including the board. Traditionally associated with risk, heat maps can be adapted to plot threat levels by focusing on two axes: intent and capability, rather than likelihood and impact,[2] which are more relevant to risk assessments. This approach avoids the complexity of incorporating consequences and focuses solely on the threat's potential.

The layout of a threat heat map typically places high threat levels (with high intent and capability) in the top-right corner, marked as red, while lower threat levels fall toward the bottom-left, progressing through amber, yellow, and green. Plotting threats accurately requires intelligence-backed justification and can be enhanced by using trajectory arrows to indicate trends, anticipated positions, and the effect of mitigation controls over

---

[1] NIST IR 8286 Integrating Cybersecurity and Enterprise Risk Management (ERM) (Oct 2020)—2.2.3 illustrates heat-map style matrices to visualize threat exposure. https://csrc.nist.gov/pubs/ir/8286/final

[2] UK National Cyber Security Centre, Board Toolkit—Risk Management & Appetite—includes examples of red-amber-green threat heat maps and discusses intent/capability vs. likelihood/impact axes. https://www.ncsc.gov.uk/collection/board-toolkit

time.[3] These control-driven adjustments allow teams to show how controls reduce intent and capability, ultimately leading to a residual risk position that demonstrates the organization's resilience.

Ten Fundamentals for Using Heat Maps Effectively in Threat Intelligence

1. **Choose Intent and Capability or Likelihood and Impact:** Decide whether to use *intent and capability* or *likelihood and impact* as the X and Y axes on the heat map. Intent and capability provide a more threat-specific focus, while likelihood and impact are more appropriate for risk analysis.

2. **Set a Graduating Scale with Clear Metrics:** Create a clear, graduated scale from high to low for both axes, such as using admiralty codes or another easily understood measure. This clarity aids in consistent threat plotting and simplifies communication with stakeholders.

3. **Collaborate with Risk Teams and Control Owners:** Work closely with risk teams and control owners to establish testing parameters, agree on threat ratings, and validate the final threat positioning on the heat map. This collaboration ensures that the plotted threats are accurate reflections of both threat intelligence and existing mitigations.

---

[3] MITRE ATT&CK® Navigator—"Layering and Heat-Map View" lets analysts depict technique frequency and control effect over time with gradient colors and trend arrows.
https://github.com/mitre-attack/attack-navigator

4. **Plot Only the Big 5 Threats:** Use the Big 5 threat vectors—Phishing, Malware, DDoS, Hacking, and Insider Threats[4]—as your primary markers on the heat map. Detail the specific techniques or TTPs associated with each threat vector in an accompanying explanation rather than cluttering the visual representation.

5. **Keep the Heat Map Clean and Uncluttered:** An overly detailed heat map can confuse stakeholders rather than inform them. Keep the design minimal, showing only the most critical data to maintain focus on the highest-priority threats and trends.

6. **Establish a Reporting and Update Frequency:** Decide how often the heat map will be updated and reported to stakeholders.[5] Monthly updates can keep it relevant for regular review, while annual reports offer strategic insights. Consistent reporting helps track threat evolution and control effectiveness over time.

7. **Leverage Metrics to Influence Vendor Improvements:** Use metrics from control capabilities represented on the heat map to inform vendor discussions and guide potential enhancements. This ensures that vendor solutions evolve in response to the organization's actual threat landscape.

---

[4] Verizon, 2024 Data Breach Investigations Report—Section 2 groups incidents under Phishing, Malware, DDoS, Hacking, and Insider actions, supporting the "Big 5" framing. https://www.verizon.com/business/resources/reports/dbir/

[5] SANS Institute, 2025 Cyber Threat Intelligence Survey (20th May 2025)—46.5% of CTI programs mapping to control frameworks (mostly threat heat maps) on a monthly cadence to executives. https://www.sans.org/white-papers/2025-cti-survey-webcast-forum-navigating-uncertainty-todays-threat-landscape/

8. **Expect High-Risk Placement Initially:** When initially plotted, threats may often fall in the red zone or near it. This is normal since the heat map is tracking active threats. As controls are implemented and take effect, the position of these threats may shift, demonstrating mitigation over time.

9. **Adapt to Stakeholder Needs:** The heat map is a storytelling tool; flexibility is key to aligning it with stakeholder expectations. Engage with stakeholders regularly, adapting the heat map to deliver maximum clarity and relevance for external teams.

10. **Link Scenarios to the Heat Map for Control Testing:** Create scenarios that align with each plotted threat to act as catalysts for control testing. Collaborate with the red team to execute these scenarios and avoid redundant efforts. Testing these scenarios provides real-time intelligence that can be reflected in the heat map's updates, making the tool a living, responsive visualization.

Enhancing Threat Heat Maps with Scenarios and Control Monitoring

The true value of a threat heat map lies in its ability to track changes in threat level over time, incorporating new intelligence, mitigation efforts, and control improvements. By linking each plotted threat to a realistic scenario (as discussed in the *Scenarios* chapter), CTI teams can work with control owners and red teams to test the effectiveness of mitigations. This practical testing allows for dynamic adjustments on the heat map, plotting threat levels as they respond to controls.

CHAPTER 21   HEAT MAPS

Visualizing Control Effectiveness and Residual Risk

Heat maps also offer an opportunity to show the effectiveness of layered controls, with each layer reducing a threat's impact on intent and capability. By plotting a trajectory of the threat's original position, each layer of control, and finally the residual risk position, CTI teams can visually demonstrate the organization's resilience. This layered approach clarifies how each control contributes to a reduction in threat impact and helps secure buy-in from stakeholders.

Cyber Threat Heat Map

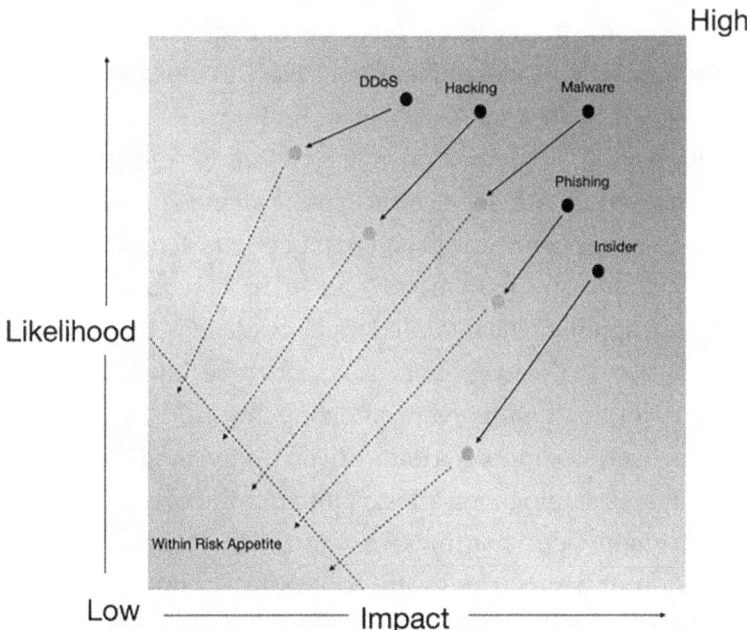

Figure 21-1. *The Cyber Heat Map in this instance using Impact and Likelihood as it incorporates Risk*

155

CHAPTER 21   HEAT MAPS

As you can see, the Cyber Threat Heat Map provides a visual analytic framework for assessing and communicating the relative likelihood and impact of major cyber threats. The horizontal axis represents impact, while the vertical axis represents likelihood, with both dimensions increasing from low (green) in the bottom-left quadrant to high (red) in the top-right. The color gradient thus reflects the escalation of overall threat severity, where green denotes an acceptable level of exposure within the organization's risk appetite and red indicates areas of significant concern requiring prioritized mitigation.

The black data points represent the *inherent threat positions* of the "Big Five" cyber threat vectors: *DDoS, Hacking, Malware, Phishing*, and *Insider*. These positions reflect the inherent threat level each vector poses to the organization with known mitigating controls or compensatory measures.

The blue data points illustrate the new post-mitigation threat positions, plotted following the implementation of specific security interventions or control enhancements. Movement from black to blue points indicates a reduction in either likelihood, impact, or both—a measurable representation of the risk reduction achieved through mitigation, thereby making the threat and risk teams more closely aligned in the process.

The dashed lines connecting each pair of points depict the threat trajectory, illustrating the path of progressive threat reduction as mitigations are applied. The intended trajectory leads toward the risk appetite boundary in the lower-left corner, where residual risk is deemed tolerable in accordance with organizational policy.

This visualization supports a data-driven understanding of how strategic and tactical mitigation efforts influence the overall threat landscape. It enables decision-makers to prioritize resources effectively, align mitigation strategies with business objectives, and maintain cyber threats and associated risks within an acceptable tolerance threshold.

Conclusion

Threat heat maps provide CTI teams with a powerful, visual way to communicate the threat landscape to stakeholders, helping track the position, evolution, and mitigation of threats over time. With close collaboration, clear metrics, and regular updates, heat maps bridge intelligence insights with risk management practices, fostering an intelligence-led, proactive approach to threat reduction. Through structured fundamentals and scenario-linked testing, heat maps serve as an ongoing indicator of organizational resilience.

CHAPTER 22

Inherent Threat vs. Residual Risk

There is a distinction between the inherent threat presented by the environment and the residual risk remaining after controls are applied.

Understanding the distinction between inherent threat and residual risk is essential for effective threat reporting and risk management.[1] *Threat* refers to an external force or action that exists independently of the firm's control—an adversarial force acting upon the organization. *Risk,* on the other hand, pertains to the choices a firm makes in response to a threat, including decisions to implement or not implement certain mitigations. These decisions impact the level of risk but do not alter the inherent threat itself.

Unlike military or government agencies, which may be able to actively neutralize a threat (for example, through offensive measures), corporate organizations generally cannot eliminate threats like APTs or state-sponsored attacks. In a corporate setting, threats are

---

[1] ISO/IEC 27005:2022, *Information Security, Cybersecurity, and Privacy Protection—Guidance on Managing Information Security Risk*—§7.2 defines inherent threat vs. residual risk in the context of control decisions. https://www.iso.org/standard/80585.html

CHAPTER 22   INHERENT THREAT VS. RESIDUAL RISK

inherent—independent of the firm's actions—and only risk can be influenced through organizational decisions and mitigations.[2]

This fundamental difference affects how threat intelligence is communicated to stakeholders.[3] By understanding that threats are inherent and unavoidable to some extent, stakeholders can focus on making informed decisions about risk management and ensuring alignment with the organization's risk appetite.

Ten Key Points to Remember When Assessing and Reporting Inherent Threat and Residual Risk

1. **Threat Is What the Adversary Does; Risk Is What the Firm Does**: Distinguish between threats, which are adversarial actions beyond the firm's control, and risk, which is shaped by the firm's response to those threats. This differentiation helps to clarify the role of CTI and informs more precise reporting.

---

[2] NIST Special Publication 800-30 Rev. 1, Guide for Conducting Risk Assessments (Sep 2012)—p. 8 clarifies that threats are external events, whereas risk level changes with "mitigation and control implementation." https://csrc.nist.gov/pubs/sp/800/30/r1/final

[3] Gartner, Communicating Cyber-Threat Intelligence to Executives (ID G00761132, 2023)—recommends separating "inherent threat posture" from "residual risk posture" in board reporting.
https://www.gartner.com/document/4016756

CHAPTER 22 INHERENT THREAT VS. RESIDUAL RISK

2. **Set a Threat Level Based on Inherent Threat:** When evaluating threats, base the threat level on the inherent threat itself—what the adversary is capable of and willing to do—without factoring in the firm's mitigations. This approach presents an unfiltered view of the threat landscape, establishing a clear foundation for risk assessments.

3. **Understand the Firm's Risk Appetite and Mitigations:**[4] Work with stakeholders to understand the organization's risk appetite and the specific mitigations they are willing to implement or accept. This understanding helps CTI teams prioritize threats that align with the firm's risk tolerance, reducing unnecessary reporting on threats outside the risk appetite.

4. **Clarify Language and Expectations with the CISO:** Confirm the CISO's expectations and preferred language around threat and risk. Aligning on terminology and understanding their risk expectations ensures CTI reporting is clear, relevant, and actionable for stakeholders.

5. **Avoid Addressing Risk in Threat Assessments:** Keep threat assessments focused on the inherent threat itself. In the "so what?" section of an analysis, focus on the threat's impact rather than

---

[4] NIST SP 1303 NIST Cybersecurity Framework 2.0: Enterprise Risk Management Quick-Start Guide
https://csrc.nist.gov/pubs/sp/1303/final

CHAPTER 22 INHERENT THREAT VS. RESIDUAL RISK

the mitigations or residual risk. This distinction keeps threat intelligence pure and focused, enabling stakeholders to make decisions about risk independently.

6. **Differentiate Between Inherent Threat and Residual Risk in Reporting**: Clearly label inherent threat levels and residual risk levels in reports to prevent confusion. Stakeholders should understand that inherent threat is an external factor, while residual risk reflects the outcome of the firm's risk mitigation decisions.

7. **Use Risk Appetite to Inform Threat Reporting Priorities**: Align the CTI team's reporting priorities with the organization's risk appetite. This approach helps avoid burdening stakeholders with threats that fall outside of their risk tolerance and directs attention to threats that matter most to the firm.

8. **Emphasize the Importance of Communication with Control Owners**:[5] Residual risk is directly impacted by controls. Working closely with control owners provides a better understanding of the effectiveness of mitigations, helping to convey how these controls affect residual risk levels in response to an inherent threat.

9. **Provide Contextual Examples to Illustrate Inherent Threat vs. Residual Risk**: Practical examples clarify the concept of inherent threat vs. residual risk. For instance, phishing is an inherent threat due to

---

[5] NIST SP 800-53 Rev. 5, Control CA-7—requires ongoing assessment of control effectiveness in order to understand residual risk relative to inherent threats. https://csrc.nist.gov/pubs/sp/800/53/r5/upd1/final

its prevalence, but the organization's decision to continue using email systems means that residual risk is managed through mitigations, not eliminated.

10. **Separate Threat Intelligence from Risk Ownership**: The CTI team's role is to inform stakeholders of inherent threats; it is not responsible for making risk decisions. The distinction reinforces that CTI's responsibility is to provide insights that help shape risk decisions, but the ultimate responsibility for risk lies with business leaders.

Example: Phishing as Inherent Threat vs. Residual Risk

To illustrate this concept, consider phishing, one of the most common cyber threats. Phishing remains an inherent threat because it is widely used by adversaries and impossible to eliminate fully.[6] Organizations must decide how to manage this threat given their reliance on email. While the firm cannot eliminate phishing, it can reduce the residual risk by implementing email security solutions, employee training, and multifactor authentication. Here, the threat remains constant, but the risk level is managed through mitigations.

---

[6] Verizon, 2024 Data Breach Investigations Report—Phishing appears in 36% of breaches, confirming it as a persistent, unavoidable threat vector across sectors. https://www.verizon.com/business/resources/reports/dbir/

CHAPTER 22   INHERENT THREAT VS. RESIDUAL RISK

Integrating Inherent Threat and Residual Risk with Risk Appetite

Communicating the organization's risk appetite in the context of inherent threats allows decision-makers to balance security priorities with operational needs. Accepting a certain level of threat while controlling risk enables the organization to make informed, risk-based decisions about its cybersecurity posture.

Conclusion

Inherent threat and residual risk form a foundational distinction for effective threat intelligence and risk management. By focusing on inherent threats, CTI teams can provide stakeholders with a clear understanding of the external forces acting upon the organization. Meanwhile, understanding and managing residual risk allows organizations to make informed decisions about the controls needed to align with their risk appetite. This approach empowers stakeholders to proactively manage risk without overestimating their ability to influence the inherent threat landscape.

CHAPTER 23

AI Emerging Technology

Investigate how AI and machine learning are reshaping cybersecurity, from automated detection systems to predictive analytics.

The arrival of Artificial Intelligence (AI) and Generative AI (Gen AI) has sparked extensive debate across all sectors in 2024,[1] with both opportunities and challenges shaping the conversation. For businesses and individuals, the difficulty lies in balancing AI's potential benefits with the risks. In the realm of cybersecurity, understanding the impact of AI is critical to adopting its capabilities for enhancing security while also preparing for how adversaries may exploit it.[2] To navigate this, it's important to begin with a fundamental understanding of AI concepts and examine how these technologies are influencing the threat landscape and cybersecurity tools.

---

[1] Gartner, Top Strategic Technology Trends 2024: Democratized Generative AI (16th Oct 2023)—discusses opportunities and challenges of Gen AI across industries.
   https://www.gartner.com/en/documents/4689517

[2] MITRE ATLAS (Adversarial Threat Landscape for Artificial-Intelligence Systems)—knowledge base of real-world and proof-of-concept attacks against ML/AI (model evasion, poisoning, data manipulation). https://atlas.mitre.org/

CHAPTER 23   AI EMERGING TECHNOLOGY

Understanding the Basics: AI, Machine Learning, and LLM

What Is Artificial Intelligence (AI)?

AI refers to the simulation of human intelligence processes by machines, particularly computer systems. It encompasses various applications, such as learning (the acquisition of information and rules for using the information), reasoning (using the rules to reach conclusions), and self-correction. In cybersecurity, AI can be employed for tasks like threat detection, analysis, and response, providing enhanced speed and accuracy.

What Is Machine Learning (ML)?

Machine Learning is a subset of AI that enables systems to learn from data and improve performance over time without being explicitly programmed for every task. ML algorithms identify patterns within datasets and make predictions or decisions based on these patterns. In cybersecurity, ML models can analyze large volumes of data to detect anomalies or suspicious activities that might indicate a cyber threat.

What Is a Large Language Model (LLM)

A Large Language Model[3] (LLM) is the product of a machine learning process, consisting of a mathematical representation of real-world processes or systems based on data. It serves as the "brain" behind AI-powered cybersecurity tools, analyzing incoming data streams to identify and respond to potential threats.

---

[3] AWS Machine Learning Glossary—definition of "model" as trained mathematical representation used for inference; security service examples (GuardDuty ML detectors, Macie). https://aws.amazon.com/what-is/machine-learning/

CHAPTER 23   AI EMERGING TECHNOLOGY

AI's Evolution in Cybersecurity: From ML to AI

AI has gained significant attention in cybersecurity because of its ability to process vast amounts of data quickly and accurately. While AI in 2024 is often marketed as a revolutionary advancement, it's important to distinguish between what is being used now and what was previously termed AI. Machine Learning, which has been part of cybersecurity solutions for over a decade,[4] focused mainly on specific tasks like spam filtering, anomaly detection, and endpoint protection.[5]

Vendors have long claimed that their solutions utilized "AI" as far back as 2013. However, it is misleading to equate early ML capabilities with today's AI, which has advanced to include more sophisticated natural language processing and context-aware reasoning.[6] AI today goes beyond detecting known threats; it has the potential to understand nuanced and evolving attack patterns by analyzing contextual data.

---

[4] Symantec, Introducing the Symantec Cynic™ AI Engine (press release, 1st Nov 2016)—illustrates early machine-learning use in endpoint security.
   https://www.zdnet.com/article/symantec-launches-endpoint-protection-solution-based-on-artificial-intelligence/

[5] CrowdStrike Introduces Enhanced Endpoint Machine Learning Capabilities and Advanced Endpoint Protection Modules (13th Feb 2017) https://www.crowdstrike.com/en-us/press-releases/crowdstrike-introduces-enhanced-endpoint-machine-learning-capabilities-and-advanced-endpoint-protection-modules/

[6] Gartner, Emerging Tech: Security Operations AI Assistants (Research Note G00796232, 2024)—documents shift from "AI-enabled" claims to embedded GenAI copilots in SOC tooling. https://www.gartner.com/document/4655345

CHAPTER 23   AI EMERGING TECHNOLOGY

The Role of Context in AI

A significant aspect of AI's utility lies in its ability to analyze contextual data.[7] Context refers to the data available for the AI tool to research, including logs, network activity, user behavior, and even external data sources such as threat intelligence feeds and open-source information. The more context an AI tool can leverage, the more detailed and accurate its outputs will be. This ability to derive meaning from vast datasets makes AI powerful in identifying and mitigating threats that may be missed by traditional security tools.

However, context can also be a double-edged sword. The AI system's performance depends heavily on the quality, relevance, and quantity of the data it has access to. An AI model trained with a limited or biased dataset may produce inaccurate or skewed results. Furthermore, using open-source data and third-party threat feeds raises concerns about data integrity and the security of the information being processed.[8]

---

[7] Google Cloud, Security AI Workbench: Bringing Gen AI to Cyber Defense (25th Apr 2023)—emphasizes the value of wide contextual data for accurate AI output.
   https://cloud.google.com/blog/products/identity-security/rsa-google-cloud-security-ai-workbench-generative-ai

[8] NIST AI Risk Management Framework 1.0 (Jan 2023)—Appendix B on data quality, bias, and integrity for trustworthy AI.
   https://www.nist.gov/news-events/events/2023/01/nist-ai-risk-management-framework-ai-rmf-10-launch

The Pros and Cons of AI in Cybersecurity

Pros

1. **Speed and Accuracy**: AI can process massive amounts of data far faster than human analysts,[9] improving the speed of threat detection and response.

2. **Automation**: Repetitive and time-consuming tasks, such as log analysis and alert triage, can be automated, freeing analysts to focus on more complex investigations.

3. **Threat Prediction and Prevention**: With the ability to detect patterns and predict potential threats, AI can help organizations take proactive measures to prevent attacks.

4. **Adaptability**: AI can learn and adapt to new threats,[10] evolving with the cyber threat landscape.

Cons

1. **Data Security Risks**: Using open-source or external data sources can expose sensitive information, and adversaries might manipulate data to trick AI models.

---

[9] IBM Security, AI and Automation for Accelerated Threat Detection (White paper, Feb 2024)—reports 55% faster mean-time-to-detect when AI analytics are deployed.
  https://www.ibm.com/ai-cybersecurity
[10] IBM Security, Cost of a Data Breach Report 2024—orgs with high AI and automation maturity identify and contain breaches 108 days faster on average.
  https://www.ibm.com/reports/data-breach

2. **False Positives and Negatives**: AI is not infallible; it can generate incorrect alerts or miss genuine threats, especially if the training data is biased or insufficient.

3. **Complexity and Cost**: Implementing AI in cybersecurity requires skilled personnel, infrastructure, and ongoing tuning of models, which can be expensive and resource-intensive.

4. **Adversarial AI**: Threat actors can use AI for malicious purposes, such as creating sophisticated phishing attacks or evading AI-based detection mechanisms.[11]

The Evolving Role of AI Vendors

As AI technology advances, cybersecurity vendors are evolving their marketing strategies. Initially, vendors promoted their tools as defenses against AI-driven threats. Now, as we approach 2025, the focus is shifting to the integration of AI as a core component of cybersecurity products, emphasizing the benefits of speed, accuracy, and automation.

Despite this shift, it's important to be cautious of vendors who claim that AI has always been a part of their solutions. While Machine Learning has indeed been used for years, equating early ML capabilities with today's more advanced AI is misleading. The key difference is that modern AI leverages much deeper context and more sophisticated algorithms to achieve higher levels of intelligence and autonomy.

---

[11] ENISA, Artificial Intelligence Threat Landscape 2023 (19th Oct 2023)—Chapter 8 details adversarial AI and AI-enabled phishing. https://www.enisa.europa.eu/publications/enisa-threat-landscape-2023

AI Use Cases in Cybersecurity

1. **Threat Detection:** Analyzing anomalies in real time
2. **Incident Response:** Automating triage and containment
3. **Risk Scoring:** Contextualizing and prioritizing threats
4. **Cloud Security:** Identifying misconfigurations and enforcing controls
5. **IAM Enhancement:** Detecting identity anomalies and governing machine identities

Agentic AI: The Next Frontier

Agentic AI systems can act independently to perform threat hunts, simulate attack paths, and trigger mitigations. Early use cases include:

- Threat hunting agents
- Security validation bots
- Remediation assistants

However, these tools must be governed carefully. Without transparency, fail-safes, and ethical constraints, they risk becoming attack vectors themselves.

CHAPTER 23 AI EMERGING TECHNOLOGY

The Role of the CISO: From Gatekeeper to Digital Trust Architect

According to PwC,[12] the CISO's role is now central to enabling digital trust. AI literacy is no longer optional—it's critical. CISOs must

- Understand where AI augments vs. replaces
- Partner with vendors offering explainable and auditable AI
- Build secure-by-design programs leveraging AI from inception

Implementation Strategy

PwC also recommends four foundational steps:

1. **Define and Assess:** Identify use cases and gaps in your current program.
2. **Select Trusted Partners:** Focus on explainability, privacy, and integration.
3. **Start Small, Scale Wisely:** Begin with high-impact use cases (triage, IAM).
4. **Invest in AI Literacy:** Equip teams to work effectively and safely with AI.

---

[12] 2025 PwC US—The AI-augmented CISO: An architect of digital trust. **PwC statistics**, such as 78% of CISOs increasing GenAI investment, and 59% working on agentic AI applications. **IAM and identity threats**, citing PwC's $13B market figure and 67% concern over attack surface expansion.

Challenges in Securing AI-Driven Systems

With the rise of AI-powered tools, there are new challenges in securing these systems:

- **Data Privacy**: Ensuring that the data used for training and decision-making does not violate privacy regulations.

- **Model Security**: Protecting AI models from adversarial attacks, where small modifications to inputs can deceive the AI system.

- **Securing Input Data**: Preventing attackers from feeding manipulated data into the AI system to produce incorrect outputs.

Five Best Practices for Integrating AI in Cyber Threat Intelligence

1. **Ensure Data Quality**: Use diverse and high-quality data sources to train AI models, minimizing bias and improving accuracy.

2. **Balance Automation with Human Oversight**: AI can automate many tasks, but human expertise is still necessary to validate findings and make strategic decisions.[13]

---

[13] US Department of Homeland Mitigating Artificial Intelligence (AI) Risk: Safety and Security Guidelines for Critical Infrastructure Owners and Operators (26th Apr 2024):—data provenance, supply-chain risk, model integrity, human validation. https://www.dhs.gov/publication/safety-and-security-guidelines-critical-infrastructure-owners-and-operators

3. **Regularly Update AI Models**: Threats evolve quickly, so AI models should be updated frequently to maintain relevance.

4. **Monitor AI Performance**: Continuously evaluate AI tools for false positives and negatives, adjusting as necessary to improve performance.

5. **Understand the Limitations**: AI is not a silver bullet. Its effectiveness depends on data, algorithms, and integration with existing security processes.

The Cyber Skills Gap and the Role of AI

One of the most pressing issues in the cybersecurity domain today is the growing cyber skills gap.[14] This refers to the widening chasm between the number of skilled professionals needed to secure digital infrastructure and the number available in the workforce. As cyber threats multiply and become more complex, the demand for trained cyber talent far exceeds supply.

What the Skills Gap Really Means

The cyber skills gap manifests in delayed incident response times, overstretched security teams, and organizations struggling to maintain even basic cyber hygiene. This shortage affects not only technical roles such as threat analysts and incident responders, but also leadership, governance, and cyber policy functions.

---

[14] ISC2 Cybersecurity Workforce Study 2024 (31st Oct 2024)—identifies a global shortfall of ~4.76 million cyber professionals and impact on incident response. https://www.isc2.org/research

Enter Artificial Intelligence

Artificial Intelligence (AI) and Large Language Models (LLMs) such as ChatGPT have begun to ease the burden. They can automate routine tasks like log analysis, alert triage, and even generate basic intelligence reports. However, they are not a replacement for human expertise.

A cybersecurity expert is still needed to

- Ask the **right questions** of an LLM.
- Interpret and **validate** AI-generated output.
- Add **contextual and business-specific insight**.
- Perform **quality assurance** before intelligence is shared or a SOC ticket is raised.

AI is a force multiplier—but it is only as effective as the expert guiding it.[15] AI doesn't replace expertise—it amplifies it. Without the right question or interpretation, even the best model can produce misguided results. This is where trained CTI professionals become indispensable.

The Gen Z Cyber Education Issue

A worrying aspect compounding the skills gap is the state of cyber education[16] for Gen Z. While digital natives, many lack exposure to foundational IT concepts, secure coding practices, and intelligence

---

[15] Microsoft, Introducing Microsoft Security Copilot (28th Mar 2023)—positions AI as a "force multiplier" that augments, not replaces, human analysts. https://blogs.microsoft.com/blog/2023/03/28/introducing-microsoft-security-copilot/

[16] CyberSeek Interactive Heat Map (US cyber workforce supply/demand analytics; updated quarterly)—shows persistent openings vs. available workers; filters by role. https://www.cyberseek.org/

CHAPTER 23   AI EMERGING TECHNOLOGY

tradecraft. Educational[17] systems have been slow to adapt, often focusing on generic IT or outdated curriculum.

Implications and the Path Forward

To close the skills gap, we must

- **Revamp cyber education** at both academic and vocational levels.
- **Integrate AI literacy** into security training programs.
- Promote **early exposure** to cybersecurity principles in secondary education.
- Highlight that AI is not an "easy button"—it still requires **skilled human oversight**.

The path forward requires partnership between industry, academia, and government. Cybersecurity is no longer a niche discipline—it is a foundational pillar of national and economic security.

Conclusion

The integration of AI into cyber threat intelligence offers immense potential, but also presents challenges that need to be carefully managed. As businesses move toward adopting AI-driven solutions, understanding the basics of AI, ML, and MML is essential. Awareness of AI's evolving capabilities, limitations, and security concerns will help organizations make informed decisions about leveraging AI to strengthen their security posture while mitigating risks associated with its misuse.

---

[17] NICE (NIST), Cybersecurity Workforce Framework & K12 Cybersecurity Education Resources (updated 2024)—calls for earlier pipeline development; integrating AI/cyber basics in secondary education. https://www.nist.gov/itl/applied-cybersecurity/nice/nice-framework-resource-center

CHAPTER 24

The Attack Surface

Define and explore the concept of the attack surface, including how to measure and minimize it to protect against threats.

This structure provides a comprehensive approach to understanding and managing cyber threat intelligence, ensuring readers are well-equipped to tackle modern cybersecurity challenges.

Understanding the attack surface is essential for protecting a business from cyber threats.[1] Contrary to what the term "surface" might imply, the attack surface is not a flat, one-dimensional space. It is a multitiered, layered set[2] of entry points, each presenting different opportunities for adversaries to gain access, exploit vulnerabilities, and cause data loss or network intrusion. The goal of cybersecurity is to reduce this attack surface, minimizing entry points that adversaries can exploit.

Attack surfaces are not only physical but also virtual, extending across networks, cloud environments, applications, and even SaaS solutions.[3]

---

[1] NIST Special Publication 800-160 v1, Engineering Trustworthy Secure Systems (Nov 2022)—§3.4.1 defines attack surface and stresses minimization to reduce exposure. https://csrc.nist.gov/pubs/sp/800/160/v1/r1/final

[2] OWASP, Attack Surface Analysis Cheat Sheet—explains layered attack surfaces across network, application, physical, and social vectors. https://cheatsheetseries.owasp.org/cheatsheets/Attack_Surface_Analysis_Cheat_Sheet.html

[3] ENISA, Threat Landscape for Supply-Chain Attacks (July 2021)—finds that 62% of supply-chain attacks exploit trust in third-party suppliers. https://www.enisa.europa.eu/publications/threat-landscape-for-supply-chain-attacks

CHAPTER 24 THE ATTACK SURFACE

The more the organization understands and reduces its attack surface, the lower the exposure to potential breaches. Identifying and minimizing attack surfaces should begin at the earliest stages of system design or project planning, as neglecting security at these stages can create unnecessary risk.

Ten Common Attack Surfaces

1. **Networks:** The network is a core attack surface with multiple layers, from the perimeter firewall to internal segments, each requiring strong access controls and monitoring to detect intrusion attempts.

2. **Endpoints:** End-user devices like computers, mobile phones, and tablets are frequent targets, especially through phishing attacks and malware. Ensuring endpoint security is essential to reduce the risk at this layer.

3. **Cloud Environments:** Cloud services, including Infrastructure as a Service (IaaS) and Platform as a Service (PaaS), present complex attack surfaces with unique security challenges, such as access control, data encryption, and vulnerability management.

4. **SaaS Solutions:** Software as a Service (SaaS) applications can increase the attack surface if not properly managed. Adversaries may exploit weak authentication mechanisms or access misconfigurations.

5. **Applications:** Both internally developed and third-party applications present attack surfaces through software vulnerabilities, insecure APIs, and inadequate patching.

6. **User Accounts and Identities:** Identity and access management (IAM) is a critical area, as compromised credentials can grant attackers unauthorized access to sensitive systems and data.

7. **Physical Devices and Facilities:** Physical assets such as servers, workstations, and networking equipment, as well as physical access points to secure areas, remain important considerations in cybersecurity.

8. **Third-Party Vendors and Supply Chains:** Third-party providers and partners may unintentionally introduce vulnerabilities into an organization's systems, creating indirect entry points for attackers.

9. **IoT and Operational Technology (OT):** Internet of Things (IoT) devices and operational technology add additional layers to the attack surface, often with limited security controls.

10. **Data Storage and Transmission Channels:** Data at rest and in transit across various networks and storage systems, especially if unencrypted or inadequately protected, is another critical attack surface.

CHAPTER 24   THE ATTACK SURFACE

Ten Fundamentals of Attack Surface Management

1. **Assess and Document the Attack Surface Regularly**: Conduct routine assessments to map and document all layers of the organization's attack surface. This includes networks, applications, cloud environments, and endpoints, ensuring visibility into every possible entry point.

2. **Prioritize High-Risk Areas Based on Threat Intelligence**: Use threat intelligence to identify the areas of the attack surface most likely to be targeted by adversaries. Focus defenses on high-risk areas, understanding that not all parts of the attack surface are equally vulnerable.

3. **Integrate Security into Early Project Stages**: Implement security measures at the design and planning stages of new projects. This proactive approach reduces the risk of adding unnecessary vulnerabilities to the attack surface.

4. **Reduce the Attack Surface by Decommissioning Unused Assets**: Identify and remove unused or obsolete assets that unnecessarily increase the attack surface. Decommissioned servers, applications, or outdated user accounts can all be entry points for attackers if not properly managed.

5. **Implement Strong Access Controls Across All Layers**: Access control is essential for minimizing exposure. Enforce the principle of least privilege and use multifactor authentication (MFA) wherever possible to secure sensitive systems.

6. **Monitor Continuously for Changes in the Attack Surface**: Continuously monitor for changes in the attack surface, such as new software deployments, network changes, or configuration updates. Real-time visibility[4] is essential to identifying and responding to new risks promptly.

7. **Establish Clear Lines of Ownership and Accountability**: Assign responsibility for each area of the attack surface, ensuring every layer has a clear owner accountable for its security. Clear accountability improves response times and reduces the risk of gaps.

8. **Apply Regular Patching and Vulnerability Management**: Keep all systems up-to-date with patches and ensure regular vulnerability scanning is performed. Unpatched vulnerabilities are one of the most common attack vectors, particularly for networked systems.[5]

---

[4] CISA, Binding Operational Directive 23-01 "Improving Asset Visibility and Vulnerability Detection" (3rd Oct 2022)—mandates continuous scanning to track changes in federal attack surfaces. https://www.cisa.gov/news-events/directives/bod-23-01-improving-asset-visibility-and-vulnerability-detection-federal-networks

[5] IBM Security, Cost of a Data Breach Report 2024—unpatched vulnerabilities cited as a top initial-attack vector, raising breach cost by $1.23 M on average. https://www.ibm.com/reports/data-breach

9. **Collaborate with Third-Party Providers on Security**: Work closely with third-party vendors and supply chain partners to ensure they follow best practices for securing their systems. Supply chain vulnerabilities are a significant concern and require a cooperative approach to mitigate.

10. **Simulate Attacks to Test the Resilience of the Attack Surface**: Run regular simulations, such as red team exercises or penetration testing, to evaluate the resilience of the attack surface.[6] Testing helps identify weaknesses and provides insights for strengthening defenses.

Conclusion

The attack surface encompasses all potential entry points adversaries can use to gain access to systems, applications, and data. By understanding and regularly assessing this layered, multidimensional surface, CTI teams and cybersecurity professionals can better secure the organization and minimize exposure. Managing the attack surface requires a proactive approach, starting with design-stage security, continuous monitoring, and strong collaboration across teams. The ultimate goal is to reduce the attack surface to align with the organization's risk appetite, ensuring that only the necessary areas remain exposed and those areas are robustly defended.

---

[6] MITRE, Adversary Emulation and Red Teaming—recommends red-team and pen-test exercises to validate attack-surface reductions. https://attack.mitre.org/resources/get-started/adversary-emulation-and-red-teaming/

CHAPTER 25

The MITRE ATT&CK Framework in CTI

The MITRE ATT&CK[1] (Adversarial Tactics, Techniques, and Common Knowledge) framework has become one of the most widely adopted tools in the field of Cyber Threat Intelligence (CTI). Originally developed by the MITRE Corporation to catalogue the observed behaviors of adversaries in post-compromise environments, ATT&CK provides a comprehensive, structured repository of tactics, techniques, and procedures (TTPs) based on real-world incidents. It was not initially designed for threat hunting or detection alone—it was a reference model to capture how adversaries operate,[2] particularly how they persist and move laterally once inside a network.

---

[1] MITRE ATT&CK®—official knowledge base describing adversary tactics, techniques, and procedures.
https://attack.mitre.org/

[2] MITRE Engenuity 18th Jun 2024—MITRE Engenuity Releases Findings of New MITRE ATT&CK Evaluations for 11 Managed Security Service Providers.
https://www.mitre.org/news-insights/news-release/mitre-attack-evaluations-managed-security-service-providers

The framework maps these behaviors across different operational stages in the attack life cycle, from Initial Access to Execution, Persistence, Privilege Escalation, Defense Evasion, Credential Access, and beyond. This granularity allows organizations to understand the full breadth of adversary activity, regardless of who the attacker is.

From Reference to Real-Time Relevance

In practice, the ATT&CK framework is more than a list of TTPs—it's a language of behavior. Within a CTI team, ATT&CK serves as an enrichment and reference tool. Analysts use it to understand what has happened in an attack, describe it in a consistent way, and compare it with other incidents. But its real power is unlocked when it is fully integrated into the CTI program.

The most effective use of ATT&CK comes when organizations overlay each attack they observe onto the framework. If ten attacks are observed in a reporting period and each is mapped to the relevant TTPs using their Technique IDs (TIDs), patterns begin to emerge. The more frequently a TTP is used across different attacks, the more it appears highlighted on the framework—often visualized as heatmaps or ATT&CK matrices with color-coded[3] frequency.

This method not only identifies the most commonly used adversary behaviors but also enables teams to

- Prioritize monitoring and detection based on frequency of TTPs rather than attribution.

- Share with the SOC a visual understanding of which techniques are most critical to detect.

---

[3] MITRE ATT&CK Navigator (GitHub)—"heat-map view" function illustrates frequency-based coloring of techniques across multiple incidents. https://github.com/mitre-attack/attack-navigator

- Focus engineering and detection development efforts on real-world behaviors, not theoretical risks.

Why TTPs Matter More Than Actors

Attribution can be a useful tool for context, but focusing solely on threat actors can be misleading. Threat actors—especially those involved in Ransomware-as-a-Service[4] (RaaS) or affiliated cybercrime groups—often share tools, infrastructure, and methods.[5] ATT&CK allows the CTI team to pivot away from naming actors and instead look at their behaviors.

If an attack is attributed to a known group (e.g., APT29 or FIN7), and that group has a defined ATT&CK mapping, then their playbook can be laid over the same matrix as other attacks. This allows CTI teams to assess

- Are the attributed attacks using the same techniques as the known actor?
- Are there overlaps with other actors' known TTPs?
- Are new or evolving TTPs appearing?

This comparative analysis is crucial for understanding shifts in adversary behavior and for identifying emerging patterns before they become widespread.

---

[4] World Economic Forum, "3 trends set to drive cyberattacks and ransomware in 2024" (22nd Feb 2024): "Ransomware activity was up 50% year-on-year during H1 2023, with Ransomware-as-a-Service kits priced from $40 a key driver of the surge." https://www.weforum.org/stories/2024/02/3-trends-ransomware-2024/

[5] Palo Alto Networks Unit 42, "The Ransomware-as-a-Service Model" (7th Oct 2021)—documents shared tooling and overlapping TTPs among affiliate gangs. https://www.paloaltonetworks.com/blog/2021/10/ransomware-as-a-service/

CHAPTER 25   THE MITRE ATT&CK FRAMEWORK IN CTI

Operationalizing ATT&CK for Detection Engineering

By continuously mapping attacks to ATT&CK and identifying which techniques appear most frequently over time, CTI teams create a data-driven picture of what really matters in their environment.[6] These insights should feed directly into SOC operations, informing:

- **Detection tuning:**[7] Focus on the most used TTPs instead of chasing headlines.

- **Threat hunting priorities:** Identify where telemetry gaps exist for high-frequency techniques.

- **Tool development:** Allocate resources to detect high-priority TIDs across EDR, NDR, and SIEM tools.

This prevents unnecessary time and resources being spent on chasing individual threat actors whose methods may not even be present in the environment. Instead, effort is focused on defending against how adversaries attack—not who is doing the attacking.

---

[6] CISA & MITRE, Best Practices for MITRE ATT&CK® Mapping (17th Jan 2023). https://www.cisa.gov/news-events/news/best-practices-mitre-attckr-mapping

[7] MITRE ATT&CK® Evaluations—public test results show how vendors tune detections against high-priority TTPs, reinforcing TID-driven engineering. https://attackevals.mitre.org/

CHAPTER 25 THE MITRE ATT&CK FRAMEWORK IN CTI

Conclusion: Make the Framework Work for You

The MITRE ATT&CK framework is not an endpoint. It is a tool for enrichment, a lens for analysis, and a bridge between CTI, SOC, and engineering. Its success depends entirely on how it is used.

When ATT&CK is

- Integrated into intelligence reporting
- Overlaid consistently across observed incidents
- Shared cross-functionally
- Updated routinely
- And prioritized based on frequency and impact

...it becomes a live operational asset—not just a reference.

It allows CTI teams to shift from actor-based tracking to technique-driven defense, giving security operations the focus they need to detect the most probable methods of compromise. In doing so, ATT&CK becomes a cornerstone of proactive cybersecurity—fueled by intelligence, refined by observation, and proven through operational output.[8]

---

[8] SANS Institute, Intellimation: Guidance for Integrating Automation in Your Cyber Threat Intelligence Program (30th Jan 2024)—demonstrates operational benefits of continuous ATT&CK overlay and cross-team sharing. https://www.sans.org/presentations/intellimation-guidance-for-integrating-automation-in-your-cyber-threat-intelligence-program/

CHAPTER 26

The Stakeholders

The success of a Cyber Threat Intelligence (CTI) program does not rest solely on the quality of intelligence produced—it depends on how well that intelligence is consumed, actioned, and integrated into the daily fabric of an organization. CTI is a service.[1] It is not an isolated function that produces reports for its own benefit. It is a capability designed to serve stakeholders across the business—some obvious, others more nuanced.

This chapter introduces the critical concept that CTI teams have dependents, not just customers. These relationships are part of the intelligence-led process, not limited to simple Requests for Information (RFIs) or reactive engagements. A mature CTI team proactively identifies, understands, and nurtures its relationships with stakeholders across both technology and business domains. Each group has distinct intelligence needs, formats, cadences, and feedback expectations. These relationships must be continually maintained, reviewed, and improved.

---

[1] NIST SP 800-150 (Oct 2026), Guide to Cyber Threat Information Sharing, §3-4—defines CTI as a service whose value depends on consumption and feedback. https://csrc.nist.gov/pubs/sp/800/150/final

CHAPTER 26   THE STAKEHOLDERS

Core Stakeholders in the Intelligence Ecosystem

Below is a breakdown of common CTI stakeholders, each with a few lines of insight into their relationship and dependency on threat intelligence.

Chief Information Security Officer (CISO): As the executive responsible for the organization's overall cybersecurity posture, the CISO expects strategic insights that inform board-level risk decisions.[2] Intelligence provided must support risk posture reporting, geopolitical awareness, and forecasting of threat trends. Cadence: Weekly to quarterly; Format: Briefings, dashboards, risk-level summaries.

Cyber Risk Management: This team consumes intelligence to contextualize threats within the organization's risk framework. They use intelligence to prioritize controls, assess likelihoods, and model impact scenarios. Intelligence must be structured to align with business risks. Cadence: Weekly or event-driven; Format: Structured summaries, risk matrix updates.

Technology Information Security Officers (TISOs): TISOs are regional or business-unit-level security leads. They bridge the business and security teams and require targeted intelligence on threats relevant to their units. Intelligence must be easily integrated into their risk assessments and planning. Cadence: Monthly and ad hoc; Format: Intelligence briefs, targeted alerts.

Cloud Architecture and Security: Cloud architects need intelligence that focuses on platform-specific threats (e.g., identity abuse in Azure, API exploits in AWS). Integration with cloud telemetry and configuration

---

[2] MITRE, 11 Strategies of a World-Class Cybersecurity Operations Center, Strategy #3 "Build a SOC Structure to Match Your Organizational Needs." https://www.mitre.org/news-insights/publication/11-strategies-world-class-cybersecurity-operations-center

reviews enhances response capability. Cadence: Fortnightly to monthly; Format: TTP alerts, threat vector breakdowns.

Security Operations Center (SOC): The SOC is one of the CTI team's most operationally dependent partners. Intelligence is used to enrich detections, triage alerts, and respond to incidents. Reporting should be actionable, tagged with TTPs, and accompanied by context. Cadence: Daily to weekly; Format: IOC feeds, analyst notes, threat actor profiles.

Incident Response (IR): IR teams depend on CTI to provide context during and after incidents—threat actor attribution, likely next steps, and tactical recommendations. Intelligence support during incidents must be real time and collaborative. Cadence: Incident-driven; Format: Live collaboration, shared reports.

Red Team/Offensive Security: Red teams use CTI to design realistic attack scenarios that reflect active adversary behaviors. The CTI team should provide regular updates on threat actor TTPs to keep red team exercises current. Cadence: Per campaign; Format: Adversary emulation reports, MITRE ATT&CK overlays.

Network Security: This team uses intelligence to harden perimeter defenses and segment the network against known attack vectors. Intelligence should include known attack patterns, infrastructure, and common misconfigurations. Cadence: Weekly; Format: Network-focused alerts, detection rules.

Engineering and Platform Security: Platform security teams need insights on software supply chain threats, infrastructure compromise techniques, and emerging vulnerabilities. CTI provides early warning and support in prioritizing patching. Cadence: Monthly or vulnerability-driven; Format: Alerts, PoC analysis.

DevSecOps: This group integrates security into the development life cycle. CTI feeds that flag threat trends in open-source components or CI/CD environments help secure the pipeline. Cadence: Per sprint or monthly; Format: Risk reviews, feed integrations.

CHAPTER 26   THE STAKEHOLDERS

Business Stakeholders Often Overlooked

Media and Communications Teams: When high-profile attacks occur, media teams may require guidance on terminology, narrative framing, and response strategy. Intelligence teams should offer situational awareness briefings and anticipate reputational risks.

Fraud Prevention: Cyber and fraud teams increasingly overlap. CTI supports fraud by identifying phishing campaigns, mule recruitment tactics, and credential abuse patterns. This intelligence prevents revenue loss and customer compromise.

Payments and Online Banking: These units are high-value targets for threat actors. Intelligence should focus on transaction fraud, account takeover campaigns, and emerging techniques for social engineering.

Lines of Business/Product Owners: Each business unit has different digital dependencies. CTI must establish partnerships to understand their unique attack surfaces and create tailored intelligence products.

Building an Intelligence-Led Culture of Partnership

Intelligence must not be imposed—it must be integrated. CTI teams should

- Understand what intelligence each stakeholder needs.
- Learn how they consume that intelligence.
- Provide reporting in the right cadence and format.
- Confirm whether the recipient has systems in place to ingest it.
- Build feedback loops into every exchange.

CHAPTER 26   THE STAKEHOLDERS

This involves structured outreach, quarterly reviews, and feedback mechanisms. The goal is not just to deliver intelligence, but to make it part of the stakeholder's thinking and workflow.

Relying on individual relationships is risky. Instead, build repeatable, documented processes. Intelligence relationships should survive personnel turnover. That requires building partnerships, not dependencies.

In closing, a mature CTI function is defined by how well it empowers its stakeholders. The team must serve as the connective tissue that binds strategy, operations, and response. A CTI program succeeds when its intelligence is seen as a critical enabler, not just a supplementary input.

CHAPTER 27

Intelligence Report Writing—The CTI Output

The output of any Cyber Threat Intelligence (CTI) team is its intelligence reporting.[1] This is the product that most stakeholders will engage with, and for many, it is the only tangible proof of the CTI team's existence and value. Therefore, it must be world class.[2]

The Art of Writing Intelligence

Writing intelligence[3] is an art that combines journalistic instinct with analytical precision. It cannot be taught in a course or captured by templates alone. The best CTI analysts possess an inquisitive nature, a clear writing style, and an understanding of the business impact of cyber threats. They know how to distill complex, technical detail into meaningful insights.

---

[1] MITRE Engenuity. "Reporting for CTI Blueprints." (7th Jun 2023) https://ctid.mitre.org/projects/cti-blueprints

[2] FIRST is the global Forum of Incident Response and Security Teams https://www.first.org/

[3] [2] Richards J. Heuer, "The Psychology of Intelligence Analysis," CIA Center for the Study of Intelligence, (1st Jan 2007)

CHAPTER 27   INTELLIGENCE REPORT WRITING—THE CTI OUTPUT

Avoiding Bespoke Overload

Different stakeholders will have different intelligence needs, but this does not mean creating bespoke reports for every team. The Request for Information (RFI) process must capture and clarify stakeholder needs early, helping avoid duplication and report sprawl. A mature CTI function should develop standardized reporting formats that satisfy most stakeholder groups.

Cadence and Format of Periodical Reporting

CTI outputs should follow a well-structured cadence. There are four key periodical reports:

- **Weekly**
- **Monthly**
- **Quarterly**
- **Annual**

Each of these should include

- A full written version (hosted on a platform such as Atlassian's Confluence)
- A shortened visual version (slide deck format)

Use the weekly reports as the foundation:

- Weekly feeds into Monthly
- Monthly feeds into Quarterly
- Quarterly feeds into Annual

As reporting periods extend, the reports should become more strategic and visually summarized through graphs, charts, and heatmaps.

CHAPTER 27   INTELLIGENCE REPORT WRITING—THE CTI OUTPUT

Pull vs. Push Reporting Culture

Foster a "Pull Intelligence" model.[4] Publish intelligence to an accessible platform like "Confluence" and ensure all stakeholders know when and where to find it. Avoid relying on email distribution ("Push Intelligence"), which can lead to missed insights.

Train stakeholders to access intelligence independently and contribute feedback through commenting tools or follow-up RFIs. Encourage responsibility on the reader.

Report Format and Consistency

Maintain a consistent structure for every product. Use clear naming conventions and headings. Articles within reports should follow the 6-article format rule to promote prioritization and editorial quality.

Each article must follow this format:

1. **Situation**: What happened?
2. **Assessment**: What does it mean?
3. **Actions and Recommendations**: What should be done?

Apply the **one-third/two-thirds rule**:

- One-third for Situation (summary of facts)
- Two-thirds for Assessment (analysis and insight)

---

[4] UK National Cyber Security Centre. "Building a Security Operations Centre (SOC)"
https://www.ncsc.gov.uk/collection/building-a-security-operations-centre/threat-intelligence

Team Alignment and Responsibility

Each analyst should own reporting for their specific threat vector. This ensures depth of expertise, accuracy, and a sense of responsibility.

- Start drafting the weekly report Monday (same day of dissemination).
- Complete 90% by Friday.
- Finalize and disseminate the following Monday, integrating any significant weekend developments.

Threshold for Ad Hoc Reports

Outside the regular cadence, major cyber events require immediate reporting. These reports should

- Take no more than 30 minutes to draft and disseminate.
- Follow a clear selection threshold.
- Be disseminated only when business impact or threat relevance is confirmed.

Conclusion

Reporting is the primary vehicle for CTI influence. From strategic briefings to tactical alerts, every word must count. Maintain editorial discipline. Build consistency. Train the audience. Enable "pull" consumption. Let your intelligence reports reflect the professionalism and operational maturity of your CTI team.

The intelligence report is not just a communication—it is a legacy. Make it count.

CHAPTER 28

Intelligence Maturity—Balancing Growth with Purpose

Cyber Threat Intelligence Capability Maturity Model (CTI CMM[1]) is a powerful and practical addition to this book. It helps organizations assess where they stand and map a path forward, keeping intelligence aligned with risk appetite, business strategy, and available resources. Below is a suggested draft that introduces the maturity model, outlines its value, and presents a structured but flexible framework that fits seamlessly with the advice and guidance within the book.

Implementing a cyber threat intelligence (CTI) function is not a binary decision. It is a spectrum of maturity that must align with the size, complexity, and risk appetite of the business it supports. Many organizations attempt to build a "complete" intelligence team from the outset—often without the right inputs, use cases, or expectations. Others remain underdeveloped, with CTI as a single analyst lost inside another function, unsupported and misaligned.

---

[1] SOCRadar CTI Capability Maturity Model (CTI CMM) All You Need to Know (30th Sep 2024)
https://socradar.io/cti-capability-maturity-model-cti-cmm/

CHAPTER 28   INTELLIGENCE MATURITY—BALANCING GROWTH WITH PURPOSE

A maturity model brings structure to this journey.

Rather than comparing organizations to each other, a CTI Capability Maturity Model (CMM) helps you assess where *you* are, where you *should* be, and what's *appropriate* based on your operating context.

It asks

- Is your CTI capability aligned with business needs?
- Is it resourced proportionately to the risk?
- Are their products being used to influence decisions?

What Is a Capability Maturity Model (CMM)?

The concept of a maturity model originates in software and process development, used to assess the sophistication of practices in an organization. It maps progression across levels, with each level indicating more structured, repeatable, and measurable practices.

For CTI, a CMM reflects the evolution of intelligence as both a capability and a service. It enables CTI leaders to benchmark growth, justify investment, and bring stakeholders along the journey.[2]

CTI Maturity Levels

Below is a simplified five-level model, adapted to reflect real-world CTI operations (see Figure 28-1):

---

[2] CMMI Institute. "CMMI Performance Solutions." https://www.isaca.org/enterprise/cmmi-performance-solutions

CHAPTER 28   INTELLIGENCE MATURITY—BALANCING GROWTH WITH PURPOSE

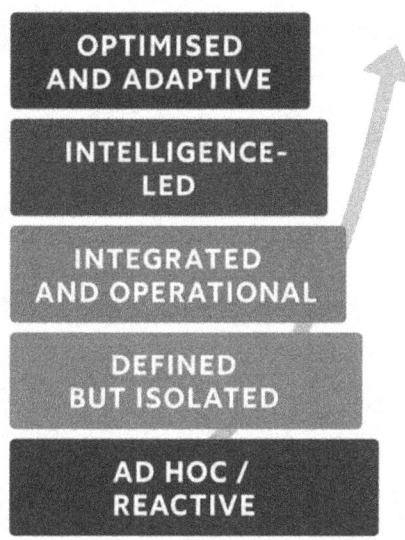

Figure 28-1. *Capability Maturity Model (CMM)*

Level 1—Ad Hoc/Reactive

- CTI is informal or nonexistent.
- Information is gathered reactively during incidents.
- No standing intelligence requirements.
- Reporting is inconsistent and often manually generated under pressure.
- No dedicated CTI tooling or processes.

☑ *Survival mode. Common in early-stage or small orgs.*

Level 2—Defined, but Isolated

- A CTI function exists, but often embedded within another team (SOC, IR, or Risk).
- Analysts may rely heavily on vendor feeds or open-source data.
- No formal prioritization of intelligence requirements.
- Reports are sporadic and audience-specific.
- Limited influence on broader decision-making.

✅ *The function exists, but impact is limited.*

Level 3—Integrated and Operational

- CTI has defined objectives aligned to business and risk teams.
- PIRs (Priority Intelligence Requirements) are established and periodically reviewed.
- Regular reporting cadence (e.g., weekly, monthly).
- Frameworks such as MITRE ATT&CK are embedded.
- Stakeholder engagement includes SOC, IR, Cloud, and Risk teams.

✅ *Operational maturity reached. CTI is seen as a contributor to risk reduction.*

Level 4—Intelligence-Led

- CTI drives proactive decision-making across cyber and business units.
- Intelligence informs detection engineering, vulnerability prioritization, and crisis simulation.
- Strong integration with DevSecOps, Red Team, and Cloud Strategy.
- Threat modelling includes geopolitical and strategic inputs.
- Intelligence is fed into enterprise risk frameworks and board-level reporting.

✅ *CTI is strategic. Respected, resourced, and embedded.*

Level 5—Optimized and Adaptive

- CTI continuously evolves based on threat trends, business change, and stakeholder feedback.
- Capabilities include automation, enrichment pipelines, AI-based analysis, and tailored stakeholder feeds.
- Threat intelligence informs product development, mergers, market entry decisions, and regulatory posture.
- Feedback loops are formalized, and quality assurance is standard.
- Performance is measured against defined KPIs and outcomes.

✅ *CTI is a differentiator. Not just good—world class.*

Applying the Model

A maturity model is not a checklist for perfection—it's a framework for reflection.

Use it to

- Prioritize investment and tooling decisions.
- Set realistic expectations with the CISO and wider stakeholders.
- Demonstrate progress in a language risk and business leaders understand.
- Avoid the "build everything" trap—where capability outpaces consumption.

Every level brings value if it matches the need. A small fintech may thrive at Level 3. A multinational bank may struggle without Level 4 maturity.

Conclusion

Maturity in CTI is not just about headcount or tooling—it's about fit, influence, and purpose. An intelligence program is mature when its outputs are trusted, its sources are respected, and its analysts are empowered to shape the way the organization defends itself.

This chapter isn't a call for perfection. It's a reminder that excellence comes from clarity and alignment, not complexity.

CHAPTER 29

The Near Future—What Else Is Going On

As we look toward the horizon of cyber threat intelligence, two forces are gathering momentum and promise to reshape the landscape: quantum computing and rising defense spending across NATO. While these topics may seem disconnected, they both demand immediate strategic consideration for those charged with safeguarding digital infrastructure, national security, and the economic engine of the modern state.

Quantum Computing: The New Crypto Threat, Without the Vendor Hysteria

Quantum computing[1] has shifted from theoretical curiosity to an emerging technological disruptor. Once scalable and accessible, these machines could render today's public key cryptography obsolete.[2] The common

---

[1] IBM Research Blog—"What is quantum computing?" (10th Jun 2025) https://www.ibm.com/think/topics/quantum-computing

[2] NIST PQC Project—"Post-Quantum Cryptography: Timeline and Impact" https://csrc.nist.gov/Projects/post-quantum-cryptography

CHAPTER 29 THE NEAR FUTURE—WHAT ELSE IS GOING ON

mantra "Harvest Now, Decrypt Later" encapsulates the threat:[3] adversaries may already be exfiltrating encrypted data, storing it with the intent to decrypt it once quantum capability allows.

But here's the critical point: **we need clarity, not hype.** Not all organizations are equally exposed, and not every system is an immediate target. So, what's a sensible path forward?

1. Quantum Safety Awareness Workshops

There's a growing case for structured workshops—aimed at C-suites, managed service providers, consultancies, and high-impact industries (such as banking, aviation, and energy). These sessions should go beyond technical jargon[4] to unpack

- What business risks are posed by quantum-capable adversaries?
- Where are the real data assets that need protection now?
- What are the investment timelines and transition strategies?
- How will governance align post-quantum cryptography with existing security standards?

---

[3] NSA, "Quantum Computing and Post-Quantum Cryptography Guidance" (21st Aug 2023)
https://www.nsa.gov/Press-Room/Press-Releases-Statements/Press-Release-View/article/3498776/post-quantum-cryptography-cisa-nist-and-nsa-recommend-how-to-prepare-now/

[4] ETSI (European Telecommunications Standards Institute), "Quantum-Safe Workshop" Series
https://www.etsi.org/events/1296-etsi-iqc-quantum-safe-workshop-2018

2. Framing "Safety" in Safety-Critical Industries

When discussing quantum-safe strategies in safety-critical sectors, we must ask: *safety for whom and from what?* This isn't just about stopping a quantum-powered attack on a sensor. It's about protecting

- **Business continuity** from algorithmic disruption
- **Customer trust** from post-breach data compromise[5]
- **National safety** where critical infrastructure or population services are involved.

Each of these has a different threat vector, stakeholder, and timeline.

3. Governance Before Gadgets

It's tempting to jump into tools and products. But leadership must first develop governance frameworks that

- Set quantum-resilience baselines by data type and criticality.
- Prioritize high-value systems for early transition.
- Align architecture, engineering, and defense operations.

Currently, we see a fragmented landscape: architects buying tools, defenders wondering how to monitor them, and business units unsure what's protected. Coordination is conversational at best. Projects will soon explode—many poorly scoped, under-resourced, and detached from business objectives. As always, **projects without a vision become time sinks. Programs**, by contrast, drive routines, outputs, and resilience.

---

[5] NIST IR 8105—Report on Post-Quantum Cryptography and Industry Risk
https://csrc.nist.gov/pubs/ir/8105/final

CHAPTER 29   THE NEAR FUTURE—WHAT ELSE IS GOING ON

4. EU and Regulatory Timelines

With the EU now recommending all Member States begin transitioning to post-quantum cryptography by **end of 2026**,[6] organizations have a deadline—not for full compliance, but for being able to show

- What systems and data are prioritized.
- What mitigation steps are underway.
- How risk assessments are documented within the organization's appetite.

Defense Spending and the Cyber Crossroads

NATO members are steadily increasing defense budgets,[7] with some projecting rises to 5% of GDP by 2030. Within this surge, cyber is becoming a headline justification. But this raises several strategic and societal questions:

1. What Is the Actual Threat to the Nation?

When politicians reference cyber as a national threat, are they speaking of espionage, infrastructure sabotage, influence operations, or corporate ransomware? The lack of specificity clouds the issue.

---

[6] European Commission—Commission publishes Recommendation on Post-Quantum Cryptography (11th Apr 2024)
https://digital-strategy.ec.europa.eu/en/news/commission-publishes-recommendation-post-quantum-cryptography

[7] NATO Press Office—Defence Expenditure of NATO Countries (2014–2024) (17th Jun 2024)
https://www.nato.int/cps/en/natohq/news_226465.htm

2. Where Is the Crossover Between Military and Civilian Cyber Threats?

Cyberattacks overwhelmingly target **private-sector infrastructure**[8]—banks, retailers, logistics providers. Yet the response is being framed as a military imperative. This raises questions:

- Will military-grade cyber capabilities ever be deployed in defense of a supermarket chain?
- Who draws the line between crime, espionage, and acts of war in the cyber domain?
- Is there a model of shared cyber readiness between defense forces and national enterprise?

3. How Does Defense Cyber Spending Translate into Corporate Reality?

Despite ballooning cyber defense budgets, it's unclear how these investments

- Support or enable private-sector cyber resilience
- Bridge gaps in public–private information sharing
- Reduce the threat burden on businesses and citizens

Currently, the overlap is **ambiguous**. A military cyber force may be highly capable, but disconnected from the everyday realities of ransomware on mid-sized firms or fraud in digital banking.

---

[8] World Economic Forum, "Global Cybersecurity Outlook 2024" <https://www.weforum.org/reports/global-cybersecurity-outlook-2024>

4. Cyberwar or Cybercrime?

The public is being sold cyber defense spending under the impression of "cyberwar." But in truth, what most taxpayers see—and suffer—is cybercrime. Phishing, data breaches, ID theft. Will the public see any of this money helping to prevent that? Unlikely. So a dislocation is forming between

- **National defense narratives** and
- **National digital experiences**

Final Thought: Aligning Vision, Not Just Resources

Quantum computing and the cyber-militarization of defense spending are not hypothetical futures. They are now active forces, influencing policy, procurement, and posture. But their value—and threat—will only be realized through **alignment**

- Between business leaders and cyber professionals
- Between military initiatives and national resilience
- Between investment and tangible, measurable security outcomes

Both domains require vision. Not reactive projects. Not vendor hype. But a coherent, well-communicated strategy that links the boardroom to the SOC, and the war room to the workstation.

CHAPTER 29   THE NEAR FUTURE—WHAT ELSE IS GOING ON

Implications for Cyber Threat Intelligence (CTI) Teams

These shifts—quantum risk and defense mobilization—are not abstract policy issues. They will reshape the landscape in which CTI teams operate. Here's how:

1. Reframing the Threat Landscape

Quantum computing introduces a fundamental change in threat modeling.[9] CTI teams will need to

- Track **actor capability development** (nation-states, academia, private labs) in the quantum space.

- Monitor **data harvesting campaigns** targeting encrypted repositories (especially in finance, healthcare, defense).

- Understand the **pre-quantum tactics** of adversaries preparing for post-quantum capabilities (e.g., credential theft for later exploitation).

CTI must assess not only **what is possible**, but **what is likely**—mapping capability against intent, and grounding assessments in reality, not vendor fantasy.

---

[9] RAND Corporation— "Preparing for Post-Quantum Critical Infrastructure" (28th Aug 2022)
https://www.rand.org/pubs/research_reports/RRA1367-6.html

2. Data Classification and Prioritization Intelligence

CTI will play a critical role in helping the business

- Identify **which data sets** are most valuable to long-term adversaries.
- Understand **where those data sets are stored**, transmitted, and exposed.
- Recommend **proactive defenses** based on the longevity of confidentiality requirements (e.g., legal documents, government contracts, IP).

This ties CTI closer to data governance, architecture, and compliance.

3. Reporting with Precision, Not Panic

CTI products must mature in how they present quantum threats:

- Avoid alarmism. Focus on **threat progression timelines**, real-world cases, and attribution with evidence.
- Provide context for decision-makers: What's the exposure? What's the adversary capability today? When does this become a budget issue?

Intelligence that supports **strategic investment decisions**—not just tactical alerts—will be more valuable than ever.

4. Supporting Cross-Domain Fusion: Military and Corporate

As defense spending rises, CTI teams in civilian organizations must

- **Map overlaps** with military CTI and national threat intelligence centers.
- Understand how military doctrine around cyber operations may influence or inform industry.
- Track whether state-sponsored tools, TTPs, or zero-day exploits are migrating into the criminal underworld.

This includes watching for bleed-over from government cyber R&D into public-domain threats.

5. Internal Threat Alignment

CTI must act as a **translator** between

- **Security architects**, who are defining post-quantum tool stacks
- **Detection and response teams**, who need to monitor or mitigate
- **Executives**, who are setting risk appetite and funding cycles

When these silos aren't aligned, tools are deployed without detection strategies, risks are logged without threat context, and budgets chase the wrong initiatives. CTI can—and should—be the integrator.

6. Preparing for Policy and Regulatory Pressure

As national and supranational regulations (e.g., EU post-quantum transition by 2026) take shape, CTI teams will need to

- Monitor legislative developments.
- Provide forward-looking threat context for compliance teams.
- Track how adversaries might exploit regulatory blind spots or transition gaps.

CHAPTER 30

Final Thoughts of Significance: Lessons Beyond the Page

As this book draws to a close, it's worth pausing to reflect on the critical but often unspoken lessons that underpin a mature, resilient CTI program. These are not necessarily headline chapters, but they form the connective tissue between people, processes, and technology. Below are a set of observations, warnings, and insights to guide your team—whether you're building, maturing, or transforming a CTI capability.

Noise, Trust, and Timeliness

- **Data Overload**: Most CTI teams are drowning in data. The real skill lies in filtering signal from noise, avoiding circular reporting, and understanding data provenance.
- **Finished Intelligence Isn't Always Useful**: Paid feeds often pride themselves on being "finished intelligence," but that doesn't guarantee relevance or timeliness. Yesterday's insight is today's clutter.

- **False Positives Damage Credibility**: One too many false positives, and your stakeholders stop reading. Trust is fragile—handle intelligence with care.

The Stakeholder Disconnect

- **CTI Doesn't Always Have a Seat at the Table**: Whether it's Vulnerability Management, SOC, or the CISO suite—many don't fully grasp what CTI can do. Your role is to bridge the gap.

- **Manage Stakeholder Expectations**: PIRs must reflect actual stakeholder needs. Regular feedback loops are essential to improve and iterate.

- **Different Functions, Different Needs**: Red Teams need simulation-based threat modeling; Cyber Threat Hunters need campaign context and logs; CSIRT wants rapid context; SOC Tier 3 requires advanced IOCs. Tailor appropriately.

Data Models, Standards, and Sharing

- **Introduce STIX/TAXII Early**: These standards offer consistency in data exchange, enabling interoperability and easier automation.

- **Dissemination Must Be Actionable**: Intelligence is only useful if someone can act on it.

- **Sharing Intelligence**: Leverage trust groups and informal peer networks, but know they're not guaranteed. Intelligence from friends is benevolence—never guaranteed like a contract.

CHAPTER 30   FINAL THOUGHTS OF SIGNIFICANCE: LESSONS BEYOND THE PAGE

The Economics of Threat

- What Is the Cost of a Breach? Average ransomware payouts continue to rise. Break it down: cost per breach, ransom demand, business interruption. Numbers focus the board's attention.

Human Factors and Training

- **People Still Click**: Security awareness training can be a checkbox exercise. Never underestimate human error.

- **Train Your CTI Analysts Too**: Use a progression model—Novice (6 months) to Expert (3 years)—with specific training goals. Match access and responsibilities to skill level.

- **Retention through Respect**: Give your team the best tools, sources, and training. If they feel credible, they'll stay.

Asymmetric Adversaries and Adaptive Defense

- **Organized Crime is Organized**: Cybercriminals mirror legitimate enterprises—with R&D, marketing, affiliate networks. They only need to succeed once.

- **You Need Resilience, Not Just Defense**: Breach is inevitable. Make resilience the goal.

- Use "What Is/So What/Then What" to guide all reporting. This framework drives clarity and action.

CHAPTER 30   FINAL THOUGHTS OF SIGNIFICANCE: LESSONS BEYOND THE PAGE

Technical Intelligence and Operational Control

- Who Owns the Tools? CTI and SOC analysts must guide the technical implementations—not engineers. Engineers build walls, but only operators can tell if the wall is being attacked.

- **Consider Attachments**: Attach engineers to operational teams for relevance. Just like military bridge-building, the tool is not the mission—defense is.

- **TIPs, SIEMs, and Integration**: All technical intel must integrate with detection pipelines. Ensure coverage and eliminate redundancy.

The SME Reality

- Not every company can afford a CTI team or even a SOC. For SMEs like Mrs. Miggins' International Flower Shop, assurance matters more than analytics. Ensure threats are seen, deleted, and the show goes on.

- Small and medium enterprises remain high-value targets, with weaker defenses, and higher stakes of downtime. Sectors like manufacturing operate on strict timelines. A ransomware attack that halts a conveyor belt costs every minute it runs idle—and adversaries know this. They bank on a quick ransom payout to restart production and meet delivery deadlines.

CHAPTER 30   FINAL THOUGHTS OF SIGNIFICANCE: LESSONS BEYOND THE PAGE

- Government services, particularly in healthcare, are prime targets, lack agile defenses and operate under the pressure of delivering critical services. The cost of service disruption is so high that paying a ransom can seem the most viable option.

- Large financial institutions invest heavily in cyber resilience, with the capacity to absorb short-term outages. Extensive investment in layered security and response plans often deters ransomware operators who prefer quick wins.

- Attackers choose targets not just for their size but for their perceived urgency to recover and likelihood to pay.

Vendor Vigilance

- **Don't Let Vendors Define Your Problems**: Vendors shape their pitch to match their strengths. Map your gaps and define your needs independently.

- **Avoid the "Self-Licking Lollipop"**: Many vendors become more about themselves than the customer. Buy based on value, not noise.

- **APIs and Open Standards**: Design systems where components can be swapped without disruption. Avoid lock-in.

- **Validate Integrations**: Ensure they work, reduce TCO, and limit alert fatigue.

- **Follow-the-Sun Isn't Just for Enterprises**: No CTI vendor delivers 24/7 support with real experts. Align SME coverage across your global teams instead.

- **Avoid Vendor Monocultures**: Don't be the next "Crowdstrike outage" victim. Herd behavior creates systemic risk.

- **SOC 2 > ISO 27001**: For SaaS vendors, demand operational maturity.

Measuring Intelligence Value

- **Track Contribution**: Which sources generated meaningful insights? Which ones produced false positives?

- **Does It Align with PIRs?** Sources should support the way your business operates, not distract from it.

- **OSINT Is Valuable—but Noisy**: TIPs and LLMs can help surface signal. Don't discard it—refine it.

Threat Hunting and Campaign Tracking

- **Hunting Requires Direction**: CTI reporting should inform hunting, not just mirror it.

- **Log Source Requirements**: Know the data you need to hunt effectively.

- **Step Sequencing**: If you know the first 7 steps of an attack, look for step 8. Understand progression.

CHAPTER 30   FINAL THOUGHTS OF SIGNIFICANCE: LESSONS BEYOND THE PAGE

Revisit the Big 5

- **The Vector Model Is Evolving**: Initial access brokers now rival phishing. Why? Because organizations invested in EDR, MFA, and anti-phishing.

- So What? Then What? Use this lens to interpret trends. Don't just describe—recommend.

Mitre ATT&CK and Attribution

- **Adopt It Widely—but Wisely**: Mitre isn't a detection engine. It's a language and mapping system.

- **Use Heatmaps**: Visualize gaps, hotspots, and detection blind spots. This drives investment.

- **Attribution Remains a Trap**: Knowing it's APT29 doesn't always change what you do. Focus on TTPs.

Conclusion

The worst thing a CTI team can be is unseen, unheard, or unused. If your intelligence isn't helping someone reduce risk, solve a problem, or make a decision, then it's just reporting.

> Be pragmatic. Be adaptable. Be a partner, not a peripheral.

If you're not intelligence-led, you're guessing. And in today's threat environment, that's not just risky—it's reckless.

Bibliography

1. The Kill Chain https://www.lockheedmartin.com/content/dam/lockheed-martin/rms/documents/cyber/Gaining_the_Advantage_Cyber_Kill_Chain.pdf

2. Admiralty Code https://www.sans.org/blog/enhance-your-cyber-threat-intelligence-with-the-admiralty-system/

3. Mitre Attack

    https://attack.mitre.org/

4. UK Government Cyber Security and Resilience Policy

    https://www.gov.uk/government/publications/cyber-security-and-resilience-bill-policy-statement/cyber-security-and-resilience-bill-policy-statement

5. Traffic Light Protocol https://www.cisa.gov/sites/default/files/2023-02/tlp-2-0-user-guide_508c.pdf

6. CTI CMM

    https://cti-cmm.org/getting-started

7. The Intelligence Life Cycle

    https://flashpoint.io/blog/threat-intelligence-lifecycle/

Index

A

Ad hoc reports, 198
Advanced persistent threats (APTs), 131, 133
Agentic AI systems, 171
Alignment, 210
Anti-fraud team, 75, 78
APTs, see Advanced persistent threats (APTs)
Artificial intelligence (AI), 14
    advantages, 169
    agentic systems, 171
    best practices, 173
    challenges, 173
    CISO, 172
    concept, 165
    context, 168
    cyber skills gap, 174–176
    defined, 166
    disadvantages, 169, 170
    evolution, 167
    implementation strategy, 172
    use cases, 171
    vendors, 170
Attack surface
    defined, 177
    fundamentals, 180–182
    stages, 178, 179

B

BEC, see Business email compromise (BEC)
Bias-free selection, 116
Big 5, 49, 221
    defined, 60
    impact and understanding, 62–64
    reasons, 60
    single-page reporting, 61, 62
Botnet, 57
Budget, 80, 107
BUs, see Business units (BUs)
Business email compromise (BEC), 50
Business sphere, 80, 81
Business's service
    critical data and crown jewels, 38
    learning, 43
    predictive posturing, 43
    preemptive control enhancements, 43
    requirements, 39–43
    response and prediction, 44
    security strategy, 38
    service and operational geography, 37

INDEX

Business's service (*cont.*)
    services and data
        prioritization, 38
    threat postulation, 45, 46
    virtue of preparation, 44
Business units (BUs), 94

C

Capability maturity model
        (CMM), 201
    concept, 200
    maturity levels, 200-204
Chief Information Security Officer
        (CISO), 15, 145, 161, 172, 190
CISO, *see* Chief Information
        Security Officer (CISO)
Cloud architecture, 190
CMM, *see* Capability maturity
        model (CMM)
CNI, *see* Critical national
        infrastructure (CNI)
Competitive collection, 111
Comprehensive training, 111
Continuous learning, 10
Cost of breach, 217
Critical national infrastructure
        (CNI), 53, 134
Crown jewels, 38
CTI, *see* Cyber threat
        intelligence (CTI)
CTI CMM, *see* Cyber threat
        intelligence capability
        maturity model (CTI CMM)

Cyber-attacks
    costs, 31
    exponential growth, 32
    scenarios, 65
Cybercrime, 210
    concept, 131
    considerations, 132-135
    ecosystem, 137
    ransomware, 136, 137
Cybercriminals, 133, 217
Cyber defense budgets, 209
Cyber fraud
    best practices, 75-78
    categories, 73
    defined, 73
    types, 74, 75
Cyber risk management, 190
Cybersecurity, 31
    AI impact, 165
    AI use cases, 171
    business, 37
    end-to-end process, 145
    goal, 177
Cyber skills gap
    AI, 175
    defined, 174
    Gen Z education issue, 175
    implications, 176
Cyber threat intelligence (CTI)
    adversaries, behavioral
        signatures, 131
    AI integration, 173
    asymmetric adversaries and
        adaptive defense, 217

INDEX

Big 5, 221
clarity, 12
concept, 45
data models, standards and sharing, 216
disruption, 19
distribution elements, 2, 3
economics of threat, 217
human factors and training, 217
implementation, 199
implications, 211–214
issues, 13–15
measuring intelligence value, 220
MITRE ATT&CK (*see* MITRE ATT&CK framework)
Mitre ATT&CK and attribution, 221
noise, trust and timeliness, 215
project *vs.* programs, 19
role, 16, 17
routine, 18
SME reality, 218, 219
SOPs, 18
stakeholder disconnect, 216
team building, 9–12
technical intelligence and operational control, 218
threat hunting and campaign tracking, 220
vendor, 107–110
vendor vigilance, 219, 220

Cyber threat intelligence capability maturity model (CTI CMM), 199, 200
Cyber threats, 32
  business impact, 195
  implications, 32, 33
  military and civilian, 209
  network and data protection, 35
  reporting, 71, 72
  scenarios, 139–143
  See also Cyber threat intelligence (CTI)
Cyberwar, 210

D

Data availability, 123
Data loss prevention (DLP), 134
Data protection, 34
DDoS, *see* Distributed denial of service (DDoS)
Defense budgets, 208–210
DevSecOps, 191
Distributed denial of service (DDoS), 57
DLP, *see* Data loss prevention (DLP)
DocuSign, 75

E

Economic threat, 217
EEIs, *see* Essential elements of intelligence (EEIs)

227

INDEX

End-to-end process
    catalyst, 149
    defensive and deception tactics, 150
    defined, 145
    fundamentals, 146–149
Engineering and platform security, 191
Engineer *vs.* operator, 25, 26
Enterprise risk management (ERM), 151
ERM, *see* Enterprise risk management (ERM)
Essential elements of intelligence (EEIs), 91–93, 97

F

Five Eyes (FVEY) alliance, 125
Fusion
    data aggregation, 85, 86
    defined, 85
    essence, 87
    strategic approach, 86, 87

G

Gen AI, *see* Generative AI (Gen AI)
Generative AI (Gen AI), 165
Geopolitics
    best practices, 68–71
    cyber threat reporting, 71, 72
    defined, 67
Governance, 207

H

Hacking, 49, 58, 60, 64, 65, 68, 93, 121, 153, 156
Heat maps
    concept, 151
    control effectiveness and residual risk, 155
    fundamentals, 152–154
    intent and capability, 151
    layout, 151
    scenarios and control monitoring, 154
Human intelligence (HUMINT), 86
HUMINT, *see* Human intelligence (HUMINT)

I, J, K

IaaS, *see* Infrastructure as a service (IaaS)
IAM, *see* Identity and access management (IAM)
IC3, *see* Internet Crime Complaint Center (IC3)
Identity and access management (IAM), 134, 179
IDS, *see* Intrusion detection systems (IDS)
Incident response (IR), 16, 139, 191
Information requirement management (IRM), 39, 42
Information security management systems (ISMS), 110

Information Sharing and Analysis Centers (ISACs), 114, 126
Informed security strategy, 38
Infrastructure as a service (IaaS), 178
Inherent threat *vs.* residual risk
  assessing and reporting, 160-163
  concept, 159
  phishing, 163
  risk appetite, 164
  stakeholders, 160
Insider threat, 11, 49, 58, 59, 65, 66, 68, 93, 121, 134, 153
Intelligence collection plan (ICP), 110
  benefits, 98, 99
  collection asset capabilities, 98
  PIRs and collection assets, 97
  strategic importance, 99
Intelligence life cycle (ILC), 8
  concept, 1, 4
  phases
    collection, 6
    direction, 4-6
    dissemination, 7
    feedback, 7
    processing, 6
Intelligence reporting
  ad hoc reports, threshold, 198
  avoiding bespoke overload, 196
  concept, 195
  format and consistency, 197
  periodical, 196
  pull *vs.* push culture, 197

team alignment and responsibility, 198
writing, 195
Intelligence sharing, 125-129
Intelligence sources
  concept, 113-117
  CTI practices, 117
Intelligence value, 220
Internal control data, 119-123
Internet Crime Complaint Center (IC3), 50, 76
Internet of Things (IoT), 179
Introspective analysis, 86
Intrusion detection systems (IDS), 35, 39
Intrusion prevention systems (IPS), 35
IoT, *see* Internet of Things (IoT)
IPS, *see* Intrusion prevention systems (IPS)
IR, *see* Incident response (IR)
IRM, *see* Information requirement management (IRM)
ISACs, *see* Information Sharing and Analysis Centers (ISACs)
ISMS, *see* Information security management systems (ISMS)

L

L3 analysts, 23
Large language models (LLMs), 166, 175

Leadership gap, 19
LLMs, *see* Large language models (LLMs)

M

MaaS, *see* Malware-as-a-service (MaaS)
Machine learning (ML), 166, 167
Machine learning model (MML), 166
Macro sphere, 82–84
Malware, 51–57, 132
Malware-as-a-service (MaaS), 51, 131
MFA, *see* Multifactor authentication (MFA)
Micro sphere, 81, 83, 84
MITRE ATLAS (Adversarial Threat Landscape for Artificial-Intelligence Systems), 165
MITRE ATT&CK framework
    alignment, 141
    and attribution, 221
    concept, 47, 183
    detection engineering, 186
    operational stages, 184
    real-time relevance, 184, 185
    TTPs, 185
    usage, 187
ML, *see* Machine learning (ML)
MML, *see* Machine learning model (MML)

Multifactor authentication (MFA), 163, 181, 221

N

National threat, 208, 213
Network intrusion, 34–36, 177
Network security, 191

O

Offensive security, 191
Open source intelligence (OSINT), 6, 86, 114, 117
OSINT, *see* Open source intelligence (OSINT)

P

PaaS, *see* Platform as a service (PaaS)
Periodical reporting, 196
Phishing, 49–51, 163
PIRs, *see* Prioritized intelligence requirements (PIRs)
Platform as a service (PaaS), 178
PoC, *see* Proof-of-concept (PoC)
Post-quantum cryptography, 208
Prioritized intelligence requirements (PIRs), 40, 76, 97, 103
    challenges, 90
    concept, 89
    EEIs, 91
    geopolitical collection, 69

ICP, 97
principles, 92–94
ransomware, 56
requirements, 89
role, 94
tasks, 91
threats, 91
vendors, 108
Private-sector infrastructure, 209
Proof-of-concept (PoC), 135
Pull intelligence model, 197
Push intelligence model, 197

Q

QRF, *see* Quick response force (QRF)
Quantum computing
concept, 205
cyber-militarization, 210
EU and regulatory timelines, 208
governance, 207
safety awareness workshops, 206
safety-critical industries, 207
Quantum threats, 212
Quick response force (QRF), 46

R

RaaS, *see* Ransomware-as-a-service (RaaS)
RAF, *see* Royal Air Force (RAF)

Ransomware, 49, 136, 137
characteristics, 54
CTI teams, 56
defined, 52
detection, 55
ecosystem, 56
growth and proliferation, 53
indicators, 55
methodology, 53, 54
PIRs, 56
Ransomware-as-a-service (RaaS), 53, 136, 185
Ransomware attack, 218
Reactive engagements, 189
Red teams, 191, 203, 216
Request for information (RFI), 101–105, 146, 189, 196, 197
Requirement brokering, 41, 43
Requirement tasking, 40, 43
RFI, *see* Request for information (RFI)
Risk, 159, 160
Risk appetite, 161, 162, 164
Royal Air Force (RAF), 45

S

Scenario-based testing, 139–143
Security information and event management (SIEM), 39
Security operations center (SOC), 10, 16, 23, 191
Service level agreements (SLAs), 110, 115

INDEX

SIEM, *see* Security information and event management (SIEM)
SIGINT, *see* Signals intelligence (SIGINT)
Signals intelligence (SIGINT), 86
Simulation-based threat modeling, 216
SLAs, *see* Service level agreements (SLAs)
Small and medium enterprises (SMEs), 28, 218, 219
SOC, *see* Security operations center (SOC)
SOPs, *see* Standard operating procedures (SOPs)
Software as a service (SaaS), 58, 177, 178
Spheres of influence, 80
   defined, 79
   observations, 82, 83
   practice, 83, 84
   types, 79-82
Stakeholders
   business, 192
   categories, 42
   culture of partnership, 192, 193
   disconnect, 216
   intelligence ecosystem, 190, 191
   intelligence needs, 196
   threat intelligence, 160
Standard operating procedures (SOPs), 12, 18, 147
Supply chains, 32, 33, 134

T

Tactics, techniques and procedures (TTPs), 48, 139, 142, 183-185
Technical intelligence
   benefits, 22
   best practices, 24
   defined, 21
   L3 SOC, 23
   operational observations, 25-29
   workflow, 27
Technology Information Security Officers (TISOs), 190
Threat, 33, 91, 131, 159
   See also Cyber threats
Threat intelligence platform (TIP), 27, 110
Threat modeling, 211
Threat vectors, 49, 93
TISOs, *see* Technology Information Security Officers (TISOs)
TLP, *see* Traffic Light Protocol (TLP)
Total economic impact (TEI), 107
Traffic Light Protocol (TLP), 127
TTPs, *see* Tactics, techniques and procedures (TTPs)

U

Unified threat management (UTM), 65
UTM, *see* Unified threat management (UTM)

V

Vectors
  attribution, 48
  Big 5, 49, 60–64
  DDoS attacks, 57
  experience, 49
  hacking, 58
  insider threat, 58, 59
  malware, 51–57
  overlapping, 64–66
  phishing, 49–51
  principle, 48
  TTPs, 48
Vulnerability management, 135, 178, 181, 216

W, X, Y, Z

Writing intelligence, 195

GPSR Compliance
The European Union's (EU) General Product Safety Regulation (GPSR) is a set of rules that requires consumer products to be safe and our obligations to ensure this.

If you have any concerns about our products, you can contact us on

ProductSafety@springernature.com

In case Publisher is established outside the EU, the EU authorized representative is:

Springer Nature Customer Service Center GmbH
Europaplatz 3
69115 Heidelberg, Germany

www.ingramcontent.com/pod-product-compliance
Lightning Source LLC
LaVergne TN
LVHW021956060526
838201LV00048B/1595